A GUIDE TO ROUGH SHOOTING

A GUIDE TO ROUGH SHOOTING

ARTHUR CADMAN

DAVID & CHARLES

NEWTON ABBOT   LONDON
NORTH POMFRET (VT)   VANCOUVER

ISBN 0 7153 6637 8
Library of Congress Catalog Card Number 74-15791

© Arthur Cadman 1974

All rights reserved. No part of this publication may be reproduced, stored in a retrieval system or transmitted, in any form or by any means, electronic, mechanical, photocopying, recording or otherwise, without the prior permission of David & Charles (Holdings) Limited

Set in 11 on 13pt Garamond and printed in
Great Britain by Latimer Trend & Company Ltd Plymouth
for David & Charles (Holdings) Limited
South Devon House Newton Abbot Devon

Published in the United States of America
by David & Charles Inc
North Pomfret Vermont 05053 USA

Published in Canada
by Douglas David & Charles Limited
3645 McKechnie Drive West Vancouver BC

DEDICATION

To the memory of my father who taught me so much about the ways of the countryside

Contents

	Foreword by C. L. Coles	*page* 11
1	Introduction	13
2	The Moorland Rough Shoot: Heather Management	21
3	The Moorland Rough Shoot: Grouse Behaviour, Blackgame, Capercaillie	32
4	The Low Ground Shoot: Partridge, Pheasant, Woodcock	42
5	Marsh and Wildfowl	60
6	Deer on the Rough Shoot	82
7	The Rough Shooter's Dog	92
8	Gathering Wounded Game	103
9	Vermin Control	112
10	The Young Shot: Squirrels, Rabbits, Hares, Pigeons	124
11	Equipment and Camouflage	138
12	Some Anecdotes	145
	Index	153

Illustrations

PLATES

Frontispiece (*By courtesy of B.B*)	
Decide first in what part of the country you want to live	page 49
Heather-burning	49
Two guns starting out	50
Most shoots have the odd small pond	50
A high cock pheasant	67
Grouse behaviour	68
Roe kid	68
A build up of geese will take place very quickly	101
A labrador is the ideal dog for wildfowling	101
My own personal choice is a labrador	102
A good working spaniel	119
Gathering wounded game	119
The art of ferreting	120
For the beginner—the woodpigeon	120

(*All photographs copyright John Marchington 1974*)

ILLUSTRATIONS

IN TEXT

1. Burning a neglected moor — page 27
2. Lighting and controlling a fire — 29
3. Butting a moor — 36
4. Siting butts on a spur — 37
5. Ageing ducks and geese — 69
6. Butting flight ponds — 71
7. Bulldozing a large pool — 73
8. Bulldozing a pool on dry ground — 74
9. Pool construction by dragline — 77
10. Basic information from deer slots — 85

Foreword

A generation or two ago most people who shot or fished were invariably good naturalists as well. The country parson, who was a skilled angler, perhaps collected butterflies: the retired colonel who rode to hounds was likely to be a keen ornithologist. A landowner who probably shot, fished and hunted, could well be forester, botanist and gardener.

An interest in country matters started young—hardly before schooldays had begun—with the finding of a first privet hawk moth caterpillar or a plover's nest. Training with rod or gun was encouraged at an early age, and with a firm discipline, whether dispensed by a stern parent or a young underkeeper detailed to take Master John out hedge-popping or ferreting with a ·410.

Nowadays our field sports tend to be divided between those who hunt the fox and do not understand shooting, and others who join syndicate shoots and regard all foxes everywhere with disfavour. Perhaps this is understandable; because so many of us have to live and work in towns, we cannot afford the time or money to indulge in more than one field sport. For the same reason many of today's urban sportsmen are inclined to be indifferent naturalists. A flock of golden plover or a marsh fritillary sunning on a wild scabious arouse about as much interest as some starlings or a passing cabbage white.

Arthur Cadman is one of those rare men in his love of both field sports and natural history. He is an all-rounder—interested in all country pursuits—and equally content with a pair of binoculars as with a rifle or shotgun. He would always be happier shooting with his own dog—trained by himself, of course—than going out without one. His professional background as a forester might be said to have given him a head start over many other professions in his knowledge of country lore, but in fact I know of all too many foresters who—I must refrain from the obvious cliché—think of little else but growing commercially desirable trees.

Arthur Cadman—and I can remember saying this to my wife soon after I first met him—would be the ideal uncle or godparent to every country boy. As to his new book—*A Guide to Rough Shooting*—which is certainly the ideal present for every nephew or godson—it also contains so much experienced advice and common sense that it cannot fail to be of value to shooters of all ages. It is full of the true spirit and feel of the countryside: the reader will also sense the excitement in the chapters on wildfowl and elsewhere. Few books on rough shooting also deal with deer, so the inclusion of this subject is a valuable one, as are the essay on the rough-shooting dog and the advice on gathering wounded game.

After much mind-searching I have at last remembered the occasion, many years ago, when I first met Arthur Cadman. We had a rendezvous in a New Forest plantation: it was a frosty morning and the stars were still in the sky. Silently we walked to our high-seats, from which we hoped to shoot a fallow buck. During the cold, cramped vigil that followed I watched the dawn come and a deer feed slowly towards me—unfortunately not one on our 'shootable' list that day. Over a dozen miles away I heard the old Cunarder *Queen Mary* hooting grumpily.

With no deer in the bag we returned to my house for eggs and bacon. Later we set out with our two labradors to walk up some little boggy pools in the hope of a few duck. In fact the total bag was one snipe between us!

I have forgotten so many days when I fired two or three hundred cartridges, but this day I remember so clearly. Arthur Cadman's book will explain why.

C. L. Coles

Game Conservancy, Fordingbridge

1
Introduction

What is rough shooting? The uninitiated may conjure up a mental picture of a line of guns lying flat on their faces, whilst some idiot looses off both barrels at a woodcock flying down the line. It is not easy to define rough shooting. Certainly it is not the big *battue*, with the pheasants streaming over in an almost endless succession whilst each gun fires his four barrels from his pair of Purdeys, aided by the slick and efficient loading of his loader.

It is the little day where enjoyment may depend upon one dog and one man, with an intimate knowledge of every yard of the ground and an accurate knowledge of the habits of the quarry, fur or feather, game or wildfowl, which may be found.

It is the rough ground, where no very large stock of any one species may be present. Variety both in terrain and in those species which are to be found, from time to time, will call for skilful planning, good fieldcraft, good dog work and hard walking.

The bag at the end of the day may not be large. Pleasure is made up of hope and expectation, fresh air and exercise, the companionship of one or two like-minded keen sportsmen, and the joy of working with one's dog.

What does the bag matter? On a big shoot I have known a day of 360 pheasants when the host and his keepers, and some of the guns, were disappointed because they expected 450 birds and because it was important to do better than the adjoining estate, which had shot 400 the week before! The bag is relative to the stock. If three cock pheasants are seen to run into a patch of rushes on the edge of the moor, where no pheasants are seen normally, and one or two are shot, that may give more satisfaction than a much larger bag on a big shoot on the low ground.

A successful day on a rough shoot is the result of good fieldcraft. A successful day on a big shoot is the result of a good rearing season and it is more a matter of organisation—efficient control of the beaters by the keepers, and skilful deployment of the guns by the host. But both types of shooting need very careful planning.

One definition of a rough shoot is an area where game is hunted, flushed and shot, as opposed to being driven. But when game gets wild late in the season, it is good strategy to put guns forward and to try to drive a wild covey, or a few pheasants or snipe or duck, over them.

Another definition is a shooting area which is not keepered. But most good rough shoots have some degree of keepering. A very large rough shoot may justify the services of a full-time keeper.

Every shooting man knows what is meant by rough shoot. To define it precisely is impossible.

The rough shoot provides opportunities for the young sportsman to learn, and for the lone shooter, and those whose purse is not up to the cost of the big organised shoot, to enjoy an outing with dog and gun. Success will come from the knowledge of the habits and habitats of the quarry, rather than from the actual shot. At the end of the day a mixed bag of a small number of different varieties of game and fowl may give more pleasure than a large bag of one species from the big shoot. In any case it is always a pleasurable duty to go over the bag with care, to smooth the feathers, sort out young from old and look for any abnormality of plumage, then hang each species in its proper place in the larder. Each bird that is hung should have a label giving the date shot, old and young being hung in different places, to avoid confusion on the dining table later. It is easier to give attention to this after a small rough day than after a very big shoot.

The perfect rough shoot will have an area of moorland, which will hold a few coveys of grouse. On the edge of the moorland

INTRODUCTION

perhaps there will be a small area of scrub birch, little bracken-filled ravines, a bank of broom and so on. Here the moorland game will meet the lowland and an occasional cock pheasant will overlap with a blackcock. Woodcock will be present in winter, a roe buck will be present in summer, and sometimes an elusive covey of hill partridges will be found. Rabbits and hares will be present. On the low ground one would hope for a few coverts or plantations, an appreciable area of agriculture (preferably farmed badly, with no crop spraying!) and an area of marshland where snipe will be found, with perhaps a pool for ducks, and a river running through it, nicely stocked with trout and, in season, sea trout. Where can such a Naboth's vineyard exist? Very occasionally in the North of England; sometimes in Scotland—but such perfection is very rare, and it is even more rare for it to be on the market.

So, he who would look for a rough shoot must decide, first, in what part of the country he wants to live. It is true to say that the man who lives on, or near, his shoot, will get the most out of it. Secondly he must decide what type of shooting he prefers. Very broadly, the choice lies between the moorland shoot for grouse and the odd blackgame and the lowland shoot for pheasants and ducks.

The next thing is to study a soil map. The most productive moorland is where the heather grows on fertile soils. Curiously enough, some of the best moors are overlying base-rich limestone geological formations. Millstone grit, which is the soil of some of the best Yorkshire moors, is excellent, too, for there is always a profusion of grit of all sizes for the gizzards of grouse, from baby chicks to adults. The best soils for pheasants and partridges are the light soils—sandy loams. The worst are the cold clays. But of course a clay soil is beneficial for making duck ponds, because water does not soak away quickly through clay.

Climate is also most important. With rainfall of more than 36–40in the head of game will fall off. Grouse will stand heavier annual rainfall than pheasants and partridges. Japanese pheasants

INTRODUCTION

will stand more rainfall than ordinary pheasants, or partridges. French partridges on lighter soils may put up with an adverse hatching time better than English (grey) partridges, but they are not happy in the hill country of high rainfall. The best game areas in Britain are where the annual rainfall is between 20 and 30in.

Topography is important, too. Warm, south-facing slopes and covers will be favoured by game much more than the north faces, which are also wetter. Deer, too, more mobile than game birds, or rather more used to travelling greater distances, need warm sunny slopes. But they will also make use of the grazing on the cold north faces which are often lush with herbage, when the dry slopes are burnt up.

With these simple facts in mind one is in a position to hazard a guess as to what any given area may be capable of producing in the broadest terms. Then comes the human factor: more and more people are causing more and more disturbance to more and more areas, formerly reasonably peaceful and secluded. Wildfowl will not tolerate disturbance and all game birds are better off without it, although birds will accept human presence to a surprising extent, provided they are not harmed. But humans imply dogs; and town dogs, running out of control in the country, are a menace to all wildlife.

Very important is the attitude of those who earn a living off the land—the farmer, the farm manager, the shepherd, forester, woodman and a dozen other workers, maybe. If the previous shooting tenant has been an overbearing, bloody-minded type, it will not be surprising if the locals have adopted a similar outlook towards shooting tenants. Once goodwill has been lost it takes a long time to rebuild it again.

One of the pleasures of a rough shoot is that one has time to get to know all those who work in the area. A friendly chat with the shepherd, closing gates that have been left open, helping the forester to control thoughtless visitors during fire danger periods—all these things, and many others, are part of country life, and the man who rents a rough shoot is very much a part of the country life of the area. Of course, it is most important to maintain friendly relations with the farmer himself, and if one can do him a good turn now and then, so much the better. He should be the first to be given a brace of birds.

Finally there is the very important matter of vermin control. Obviously, if the rough shoot is surrounded by well-keepered properties, not only will there be much less vermin, but there will also be a greater head of game in the general region. Unfortunately, most rough shoots are situated in areas where there has been little or no vermin control.

A large rough shoot may justify the employment of a full-time keeper, but to my way of thinking this raises the status above that of a true rough shoot. On the other hand, every rough shoot will benefit from some part-time keepering, whether this be heather-burning, vermin-killing, or feeding flight ponds and putting out food for pheasants and partridges. A pleasure of living near one's shoot is to be one's own part-time keeper. More time spent there means more personal knowledge of the area, and the sport will benefit as a result.

It is also most important to make contact with the keepers on adjoining estates. To help one another is a simple creed, and in the long run pays. Always respect the march fences meticulously and let it be obvious that you do not harry those birds which have wandered on to your side of the boundary. Above all do not shoot hen pheasants late in the season, just because they are your neighbour's.

It is essential to know the exact march or boundary of one's shoot on all sides. This knowledge is vital to every member of a syndicate, if the shoot is shared with others. Apart from the fact that one does not want to trespass, it is most necessary to know the boundary when one is planning a day's shooting. Indeed, it is a great advantage to have a good idea of what sort of country lies over the boundary. If there is a tempting field of roots, or area of rough, care must be taken to work one's birds away from this temptation, and not towards it—or one may lose half one's stock over the march in the first two hours of the day.

Description of a few actual rough shoots will illustrate the extremes of the whole range. The first was at Minster Lovell, a delightful little village in Oxfordshire. That was a long time ago in my undergraduate days. Three of us shared the shoot and paid next to nothing for it. There were three large arable fields, and a few fields of pasture, a rough bank with wild roses and thorn bushes, a small larch wood and—the main interest to us— a large marsh through which the river Windrush flowed. What tremendous enjoyment we drew from this little paradise! The arable and pastures produced three partridge drives, two down-wind and one return, for our three coveys of partridges. The large wood held a few pheasants and hares, and many pigeons. The marsh held some snipe, a few pheasants and always a duck or two. It was here that I experienced the magic of duck flighting for the first time. The whole shoot provided an afternoon's sport and if the bag reached double figures it was quite something.

Another example is one which Eric Stevens and I took: Meall Dubh—6,000 acres of fresh air and exercise in the Highlands of Scotland. It is a vast expanse of heather and deer grass and rock, rising from 800ft to just under 2,600ft, with probably more than half of it entirely unproductive. But there are some grouse, and, on the grey, rock-strewn tops, some ptarmigan, those most beautiful of all game birds. On 14 August three of us (with three retrievers, one sheepdog and a terrier) walked many miles and shot six brace of grouse and four and a half brace of ptarmigan. I doubt if I have ever enjoyed a day's shooting more, for the magnificent scenery and those beautiful birds whirling away from the grey rocks, like large white moths against the distant navy-blue hills, left a memory that will remain with me for ever. Also, just to top up a splendid day, a golden eagle, with his vast wingspread, swept regally across the hill as we made our way down.

Then there was the duck marsh in Wales. Here the mountain torrent ran sluggishly through a very large area of flat bog-land, the course of the river being flanked by rushes, which became partly waterlogged in winter. Parts of the area were so level that the river opened out into wide shallow 'pans' or flashes, some three gunshots in width and many more in length. Our small shoot held one of these flashes and three-quarters of a mile of river, together with a small isolated pond and many acres of rushy bog. Around the farm were one or two fields of oats and some wet pasture. Game was scarce. In a good year there might be one fair-sized covey of partridges and two broods of pheasants.

But many broods of mallard were reared there. In winter, the main flash was used by large packs of wigeon and teal, and, most exciting of all, the Greenland whitefronts. These beautiful geese would use the flash whenever the moon was full and sometimes at other periods. When the weather was rough a morning flight would produce forty head, and at one time or another almost every species of duck has been recorded. Snipe were always present, though not in large numbers. As with all wildfowl shoots, one of the main pleasures was the unexpected red-letter day. One morning the geese poured into the small pool and two of us, crouching in the rushes, shot seven in a wonderful twenty minutes. The last morning flight I had there was an all-time record, for a tremendous mallard flight took place, and I picked twenty-nine ducks to my own gun. Normally, two or three ducks and a couple of snipe would be all that a party of three or four guns could expect.

We had great fun making butts, even though all the materials had to be carried a very great distance. The outstanding one was an enormous sunken tub which had to be rolled for the full length of the bog and sunk in a great hole which we dug. When the first winter flood came this huge barrel shot out of the ground like a cork out of a bottle. It had to be re-fixed with three 9ft iron bars driven obliquely into the bog and bolted to the flanges. After that, a plastic bucket was an essential piece of equipment. (A metal bucket made too much noise when baling out the floodwater.)

As a complete contrast to the rough duck shoot there is the all-woodland shoot. Whilst small woods are an enormous asset to any shoot, whole large blocks of woodland, without any

INTRODUCTION

arable land, are the most difficult. Here one's main quarry is likely to be roe, to be stalked with a rifle at dawn on a summer morning, or woodcock in winter, with an occasional pheasant or blackcock. Pigeons will be the most numerous quarry and a great deal of careful planning is needed to make the most of them. Suitably placed high seats are often necessary for both roe and pigeons. On one such shoot where two or three head was the normal bag, two of us were once lucky enough to encounter a fall of woodcock. In two hours we picked thirteen and lost one more.

Every rough shoot will prove to be more suitable to one or other of the game and fowl species. Generally speaking, it is better to promote the welfare of those species which already exist rather than introduce others. But if it is desired to introduce other species, then the first step must be to find out why they are not already present, and then to produce suitable habitats. Only after that can one hope to succeed.

In these days the threats of ever-increasing pressures upon our countryside and shores, of more and more agitation by the anti-blood-sports fraternity, even of misguided legislation drafted by civil servants with no knowledge of field sports, are very real. Every sportsman should belong to one, or all, of the organisations whose objects are to safeguard and enhance field sports.

The Wildfowlers Association of Great Britain and Ireland (WAGBI) for shooting—all shooting, not just wildfowl—and conservation, the British Field Sports Society (BFSS) and the Game Conservancy all deserve full support, not for what one can get out of them but to aid the excellent work that they do in the interests of shooting people.

2
The Moorland Rough Shoot: Heather Management

There are very few rough shoots which will have the good fortune to hold ptarmigan, for these birds live only above the 2,000ft contour in parts of the Scottish Highlands. Their worst enemies are the eagle, the hoodie crow and the fox, and control of the last two on the high ground will help the stock to increase. They are exceptionally hardy birds and there is nothing I can suggest which will improve their conditions, for the vegetation is too sparse to burn successfully. However, when they have had a good breeding season it is important to reduce the number enough to leave a healthy breeding stock compatible with the area of suitable habitat, and the food supply thereon. This principle applies to all game from deer downwards.

Quite often there will be a conflict between the interests of stalking and those of shooting on the high ground, as red deer, ptarmigan and grouse all share the same region and may overlap to some extent. In a good deer forest, stalking interests must come first, but it should be possible to arrange some shooting days for ptarmigan and grouse, especially early in the season.

Some moorland which holds a stock of grouse will occur on many rough shoots in the north of England and much of Scotland and also in some localities in Wales and Ireland. When this is so, it is very rare to find an area which cannot be improved. Indeed local inquiry will often produce some information about the bags of grouse in previous times, which will indicate that the moor once carried a much greater stock than today. It is important to assess the reasons for the decline, although usually they are not far to seek, since the grouse stock will fall off in direct proportion to the degree of neglect of proper moor management.

Curiously enough, it will be found very frequently in Scotland that there is a similar decline in the number of blue hares, a well-burnt moor being more favourable to blue hares than many acres of coarse heather. There is also some benefit in allowing a reasonably numerous stock of blue hares to build up on a moor. The beneficial reasons are threefold. First, foxes, wild cats and eagles prefer hares to grouse, or perhaps they find them easier to kill. At any rate there will be less mortality from predators amongst the stock of grouse where hares (and rabbits) are available for food for the predators. Second, during periods of snow the hares (now white, of course) scratch through the snow and make it easier for grouse to reach the heather. Red deer have a similar effect. Finally, on the very high ground, where burning is extremely difficult if not impossible, hares prune the clumps of heather and to some extent reduce the need to burn.

The first thing to put right on a neglected moor is the heather. In nearly every rough moorland shoot the heather will have been inadequately burnt and in most cases it will be just one vast area of old heather. However, exceptionally, especially where there is a high stocking of sheep, the heather may have suffered from over-burning. This is just as disastrous as under-burning.

Grouse require all age classes of heather to be present, with a preference for young heather, which provides the most suitable and most nutritious food. Some old heather is essential for nesting cover and for winter feed when snow may lie to some depth over young heather, although grouse will burrow under the snow to reach suitable food.

People who know the moor only during the period immediately after the Twelfth find it hard to believe that there can be a shortage of heather for grouse food. 'Look, there are thousands of acres of heather. You can't tell me that there's not enough for every grouse that has ever been hatched,' say the August visitors. Let them walk over the same ground in March after a late, cold spring and searing east winds. The heather will appear black and one may have to search on hands and knees for several yards before one single green shoot, suitable for a grouse to eat, can be found. The lean time for all game is January–March and sometimes April. That is when the red deer die—not during the storms of mid-winter. That is when the success of the next grouse-shooting season is decided. If the heather has come through the winter reasonably well (assuming sufficient of the right ages), then the grouse will be in good condition. If the breeding pairs are in good condition when they nest, the eggs will be more fertile, and the young more viable, than they will be if the breeding birds have wintered badly. This factor is of greater importance than any other, including the weather at hatching time. It is impossible for breeding birds which are in poor condition to produce good results, however favourable all other subsequent factors may be.

Therefore it is imperative to ensure that the heather of the moor is in the optimum possible condition for the health of the grouse stock.

A well-managed moor will present the appearance of a patchwork quilt, as a result of burning very many small patches in rotation over many years. Our rough moorland shoot is most unlikely to fall into this category. It will probably be a sea of unbroken heather of considerable age. At once one will be tempted to organise a few large fires. But this is not the answer, for the very simple reason that a large fire eliminates all possible nesting cover and therefore the burnt area will be sterile for grouse production for several years. Burning must be done in small patches, but the practical difficulty is how to achieve this *safely*, because few moors are entirely isolated from some hill forestry somewhere, and a heather fire which gets out of control can spread over several miles very rapidly.

Let us assume that our rough moorland shoot presents us with the very common problem of getting many hundreds of acres of unburnt heather into proper condition. How do we set about burning? First it is necessary to understand something of the complexity of a moorland fire.

There are three main factors which govern the way in which a fire behaves. First, humidity. Obviously, soaking wet vegetation will not burn at all, and wetness depends on the weather and the humidity of the atmosphere. If the heather is damp in the bottom but dry on top it will not burn well, and, if it burns at all, a clean burn will not be achieved. But if it is dry in the bottom and damp on top, a condition which is quite frequent in dry weather, early in the day, because the night's dew or frost will have dampened the top, then it will burn. The fire will be slow to start, but, as a hot front to the fire develops, the moisture will be dried in front of the fire, which will burn even more quickly.

The second factor is the texture of the heather. Short, open heather will not burn very readily, and indeed one does not wish to burn this type of heather. Dense, tall heather will burn most fiercely. Very old coarse heather, which has gone thin through age, will not burn quite so easily. Dry *Molinia* (ribbon grass) mixed with heather will burn very rapidly.

The third factor, and the most important one, is wind. Wind force and wind direction are of paramount importance and both may change unexpectedly. It is the unforeseen change in the wind which is the most frequent cause of a controlled fire getting out of hand and causing a disaster. Very often there may be little or no wind early in the day, but as the sun warms the ground the air rises, and this is the start of a wind which may gain in strength during the course of the day. A variable wind of moderate strength may be more dangerous than a strong but steady wind.

With these basic facts, one should next consider which of the areas adjoining the moor are vulnerable and which are safe. Vulnerable areas are (a) forests, and (b) adjoining moorland or heathland grazings with gorse, heather, *Molinia* or other dry grass and of course buildings and fences. If the forest has a clean floor (ie if the trees have reached a sufficient age and size to kill out the ground vegetation by shade) or if the adjoining moor is well burnt and has no large areas of old heather, the problem is simplified. But it must still be taken seriously. Areas that are safe are fields of pasture or arable (as opposed to rough grazing, which may be inflammable).

In between these two extremes (vulnerable areas and safe areas) there will be varying degrees of danger—dense gorse is perhaps the worst—and reasonable safety, such as streams, roads, paths and grassy areas. If grassy areas have been well grazed they will be reasonably safe, that is, a fire will creep only slowly across and can be controlled easily. Rushes (*Juncus*) will check a fire, because they are green in the bottom, but a fierce fire may sweep over the dry tops. The stronger the wind, the fiercer the fire and the greater the danger of such a fire 'jumping' the safe gap. *Molinia* and gorse fires are more liable to jump than heather, the cause being burning fragments carried across the safe barrier. This is because gorse is higher than heather and burns with a greater heat, emitting sparks from a higher level. *Molinia* is so light that burning ribbons become airborne.

All these points must be borne in mind before any burning is started.

Burning must be carefully planned. Although ideally a well-burnt moor should be composed of many small isolated fires, each not more than a chain wide (ie the length of a cricket pitch), which will produce heather of different age groups according to when each patch was burnt, it is wrong to attempt to achieve this during the first year or two on a moor where burning has been neglected. Every small patch which is lighted in isolation is a risk.

It is far better to burn strips one chain wide for the greatest possible length. Such strips serve a dual purpose. First, they make a continuous firebreak from which future fires can be lighted. Second, the line will cross through a number of territories of different pairs of grouse which like to nest in the long heather within reach of the young heather, which will grow on the burnt areas. Although this young growth will not be ideal until after the second or third year's growth, a freshly burnt area is still of value for baby grouse to come out to dry themselves after rainfall. Indeed, in wet weather adult grouse prefer open ground. In dry weather they like to be able to dust.

So, in the first year or so the aim should be to split up the moor by long continuous burns. These should not exceed two chains in width and the aim should be about one chain in width but as long as is convenient.

Figure 1 shows an example of an unburnt moor, with a forest to the north, another moor to the south-west and fields to the east and south. The first object must be to split it up into manageable areas, and this must be done in the first year. There are several ways to achieve this, according to wind direction.

1 If the wind is in the west, it would be wise to back-burn a strip from the fields to the lunch hut, and another strip beside the stream. If it does get out of hand it will burn out on the fields and the Land Rover road will provide a measure of safety on the flank. Subsequently this line can be continued to the south-west to link up with the nearest burnt area on the neighbouring moor. The stream will provide a measure of protection on the flank.

2 With a light north wind the aim should be to strengthen the break made by the Land Rover road by burning on the east side of it. A decision must be taken whether to burn down-wind, which is much quicker, or up-wind. As the wind is away from the forest a down-wind burn is possible, provided weather conditions are not too hazardous. A strip should be back-burnt adjoining the next moor. A small back-burn could be attempted in block E from the stream.

3 With a south wind, a back-burn on the south-west side of block D will make this block safe for patch-burning next year. Very careful small back-burns should be done from the forest fire trace, *provided* this is not attempted in a strong wind or very dry conditions.

4 An east wind will give a chance to start a back-burn at the junction of the safe field with the forest. At first, this fire could be taken obliquely, because the burnt area on the next moor will be safe, but it must be turned directly into the wind

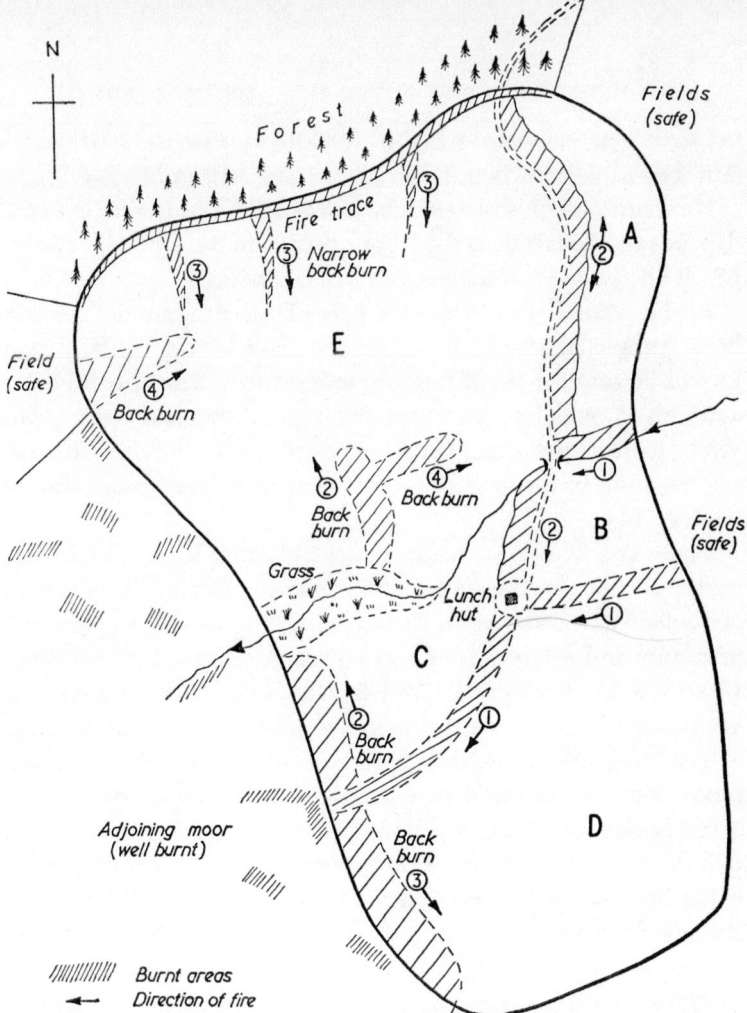

Fig 1 Burning a neglected moor. The arrows show the directions taken by the fires—normally up-wind unless the wind is light and the area quite safe

First year
1. West wind. Back-burn only, to form long strips.
2. North wind. Burn break alongside road. This is possible down-wind if wind is not strong.
3. South wind. Back-burn along march fence in Block D. Very carefully back-burn narrow strips from fire trace by forest.
4. East wind. Back-burn from field in western part of Block E, obliquely at first, then turning into wind. Back-burn from (2) in Block B.

Second year
Continue to break up Block E with long narrow strips whenever conditions are safe. Patch-burn in Blocks A, B, C and D.

Third year
Continue. Some patch-burning in Block E should be possible.

before it gets beyond the end of the safe area on the next moor. Another back-burn is possible from burn two in block E.

How much of this programme can be achieved in the first year depends on the weather, the labour force and the wind directions. But it shows the general pattern to be aimed at.

In the second year, whatever part of the programme has not been completed should be attempted. But blocks A, B, C and D will be safe for patch-burning subject to normal precautions, and this should be the target for the second and subsequent years. At the same time, whenever conditions are favourable for safe burning in block E, the most dangerous area, more should be done here.

There are, of course, many alternatives to what has been suggested above, and Figure 1 is intended only as a broad guide. In fact adequate burning is a matter of seizing every available opportunity and using caution and common sense. There are times when a bold course is safe and then it is right. But always it is essential to be alert to any possible change in wind and weather.

The foregoing covers the broad strategy of burning a neglected moor. But the practical problem of how to light and control a fire is also of paramount importance. On the big moor there will be men of experience to carry out the burning, and the better it has been burnt, the easier is the task. On the rough moorland shoot it is probable that no one will have much experience and because of neglect the risk is very much greater. It is necessary to know how a fire behaves. Figure 2 shows (I) the development of the heather fire and (II) how to back-burn. At the point of ignition (I_1) the first little candle-sized flame may be struggling to get going. At this stage a small infant can put it out. Do not be fooled by this; soon it will be crackling and sparking over a square foot (I_2). Anyone can still extinguish it. Quite quickly it will become an oval, a yard wide, with the centre of the circle blackened and burnt out and the front taking hold (I_3). If one is wanting to make a burnt firebreak, now is the time to extinguish the down-wind half of the circle so that a number of such circles treated this way will soon make a rough line

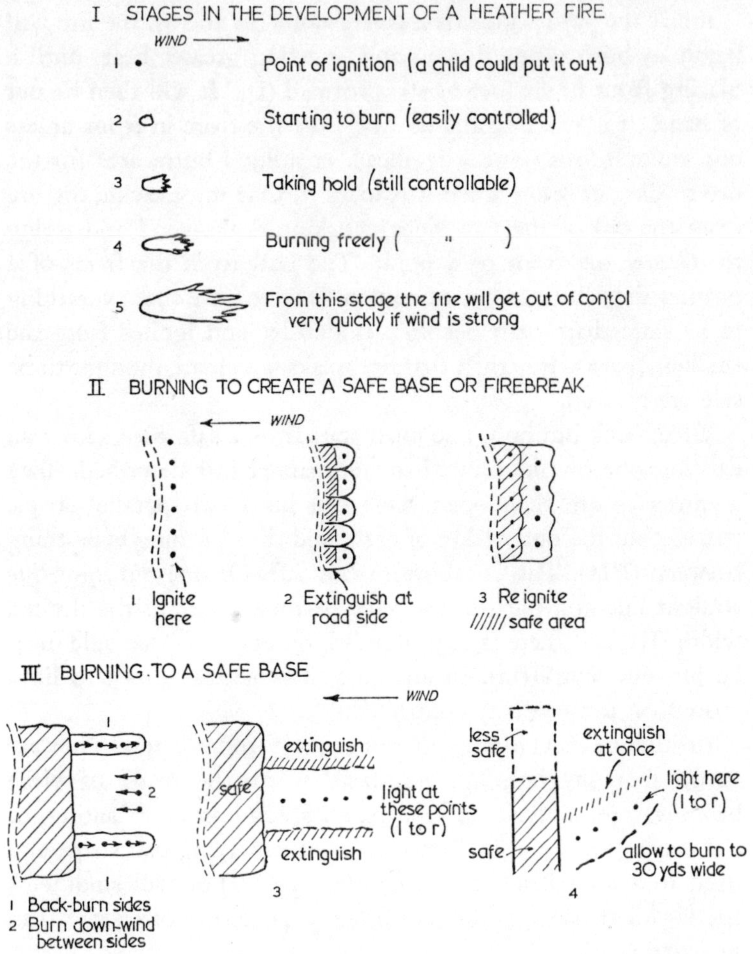

THE MOORLAND ROUGH SHOOT: HEATHER MANAGEMENT

I STAGES IN THE DEVELOPMENT OF A HEATHER FIRE

WIND ⟶

1 • Point of ignition (a child could put it out)

2 ○ Starting to burn (easily controlled)

3 ⌒ Taking hold (still controllable)

4 ⌒ Burning freely ("   )

5 ⌒ From this stage the fire will get out of contol very quickly if wind is strong

II BURNING TO CREATE A SAFE BASE OR FIREBREAK

⟵ WIND

1 Ignite here   2 Extinguish at road side   3 Re ignite ////// safe area

III BURNING TO A SAFE BASE

⟵ WIND

1 Back-burn sides
2 Burn down-wind between sides

3 safe / extinguish / light at these points (l to r) / extinguish

4 less safe / safe / extinguish at once / light here (l to r) / allow to burn to 30 yds wide

Fig 2 Lighting and controlling a fire

with the down-wind side out (II2), the other side slowly burning into the wind. By relighting another series of small fires one or two yards farther up-wind (II3), the 'dead' line can be widened as the new fires burn into it. When a perfectly safe base has been made, a much wider area can be lit to burn down-wind into the safe area.

But if the yard-wide circle is left alone (I3 and 4), the fire will begin to burn faster down-wind, creating greater heat, until a blazing front of six feet or so is formed (I5). It will then be out of hand. It is not possible to tackle the fire from in front unless one counter-fires some way ahead, creating a burnt area for the fire to die out upon when it reaches it. One must tackle the fire from the tail of the two sides, working down-wind and trying to narrow the front to a point. The heat from the front of a heather fire which is out of control is so intense that everything in its immediate path becomes tinder-dry and ignites from the smallest sparks. It is then that firebreaks which are thought to be safe are crossed.

When back-burning, one must start from a safe base, either an existing one or one created in the manner just described. Two alternatives are then open. One can burn two parallel strips, putting out the outer edge of each, and then burning everything between (III1). This is laborious but safe. Or one can light one straight line and put out the sides as they widen to the desired width (III3). If there is a greater risk on one side, that side must be put out first (III4). In any case, it is necessary not to light more than can be easily controlled.

Heather burners can be bought at most ironmongers. They are useful for easy lighting. Fire-beaters may be made of birch brooms, light shovels on long handles, old conveyor belting, or old netting bent and tied into a sort of flat frying-pan shape and fixed to a long handle. I prefer this type. They will smother a fire if you stroke it firmly, with less expenditure of energy than in actual beating.

I have covered this problem of burning in some detail, most of it elementary. But it *is* a problem and it *has* to be tackled. Perhaps it is more important to get a small rough moorland shoot well burnt than a bigger one, when some neglected areas can be absorbed in the whole. But no one can afford to be complacent when burning. There is the story of the young keeper burning for the first time. He was left in charge of a safe fire to watch it and gain experience. An hour later the head keeper came over to see how he was getting on. 'How's it going?' he asked. 'Fine,' said the young keeper, looking very busy in his shirt sleeves, 'I've hardly had to do a thing.' 'What's that brown thing smouldering away in the middle?' asked the head keeper. It was the young man's jacket.

3
The Moorland Rough Shoot: Grouse Behaviour, Blackgame, Capercaillie

The main food of grouse is ling heather (*Calluna*) and, as already stated, they need a sequence of age classes of heather, three-year-old providing the best food. They also eat bilberry (*Vaccinium*) leaves, flowers and berries, and all the other moorland berries in season. The heath (or moorland) dwarf rush (*Juncus squarrosus*) is a favourite food when the seeds are ripe in September. The young eat insects for the first ten days or a fortnight, after which they change to heather tips. Oats are eaten freely when fields of oats are reasonably close to the edge of the moor. Grouse drink every day, but much of this need is fulfilled by dew. However, a dry, south-facing moor may suffer from drought in a very dry year, and then the wetter ground will carry a greater stock. In a wet season the reverse will be the case. It is beneficial to open up small pools as drinking-places, wherever possible, on dry ground.

All grouse need grit. Sharp quartz grit from about the size of the diameter of a grain of wheat to the length of half a grain of wheat is needed in the gizzard in order to grind the heather shoots. The greatest need is in winter and early spring, when the heather is more coarse than in the growing season. Therefore it is necessary to put out grit on bare ground before winter comes. A single furrow ploughed where the soil is not deep peat will provide some grit and also dusting-places.

It is important that the following points should be known and understood.

1 Moors which carry the highest stock of grouse are those situated on base-rich rocks, because the heather is more nutritious, and those where the heather has been burnt properly.

2 Good breeding success depends on the condition of the parent birds at nesting time, and that in turn depends on the condition of the heather, first the growth in the previous summer, and second the condition at the end of the winter. Birds in poor condition cannot produce large broods.

3 Territorial behaviour begins in August, when the most aggressive cocks start to take up their territories. The family coveys tend to split up in September and October. Packs are formed of cocks without territories and hens. Then they are wild and difficult to shoot by walking up. The more stormy the weather the earlier they form packs.

4 October is the main month for the complete formation of territories. Hens move to form pairs with cocks in possession of territories. The activity takes place in the early morning; later in the day the birds are in their normal packs. But the territories are defined. There is a very considerable surplus of birds without territories. These may be 65 per cent of the stock.

5 From January to April pairs are in their territories continuously. Occasionally one cock will have two hens, both nesting.

6 The main predation is on surplus birds, and very few of the surplus birds will survive after April. Those that escape predation die of stress, parasites or starvation.

7 During the nesting season, April to July, very little will be seen of the breeding birds. The fewer birds that are seen, the better the prospects of a good season, for those that move freely are barren birds, mostly, and many barren birds indicates a poor season.

8 Grouse are short-lived, not many living beyond two years. Ringing has not yet shown any evidence that grouse migrate. Certainly the majority of grouse do not move more than two or three miles. The stock on a moor that is neither shot nor managed will deteriorate very fast.

It is quite clear from all these facts that it is better to shoot a moor hard than too lightly, because the large number of surplus birds should be harvested. But in a good season it is very difficult to shoot enough birds in the relatively short time available.

There are three methods of shooting grouse: dogging, walking up, and driving.

Dogging—shooting over pointers or setters—is a very exciting and enjoyable form of sport, the pleasure being as much from watching the dogs work as from shooting. Walking up is a method most suitable for the outlying areas and the edge of the moor.

Both methods have disadvantages for the future of the moor. Barren birds and single old cocks tend to escape, because they rise farther away than do the coveys of young birds. But when driving, it is the old birds that are shot more easily. Often, when there are late broods, the parent birds present an easy shot and are killed by walking up guns before the small brood is ever seen. Without their parents the young are liable to die. When driving, these parent birds survive, because they swing round and return to their young, and do not fly over the butts.

The period when birds will lie well is very limited and it is impossible to kill enough birds in a good season. Therefore moors which are consistently shot by dogging, or by walking up, only, will very rarely become first-class moors or produce the large bags which moors shot by driving will produce.

For this reason it is important to be prepared to drive grouse even on the rough shoot. In fact, when grouse have become too wild to walk up, it is the only method which will produce results. Therefore the main principles which govern driving grouse should be understood even by the rough shooter. The bag is relative to the stock of birds on the ground. Perhaps in the case of the small moorland rough shoot it is a case of 'ambushing' a covey or two of grouse by the simple expedient of three or four guns being stationed on a suitable flight line, and two or three guns working their dogs, accompanied by three or four beaters, moving the birds forward. When it succeeds it can be most enjoyable. To succeed with but few beaters, few birds and few forward guns requires a high degree of skill and great knowledge of the ground.

Let us therefore look at the main rules for driving grouse.

The first drive must be down-wind. How often one sees the whole day ruined because this simple rule has not been observed. This happens either because it is not convenient to alter the routine, which may depend on lunch in one place only, and the least possible walking for the guns. The simple reason for this rule is that grouse cannot be pushed far up-wind away from home. But if they have first been moved down-wind they will be willing, even eager, to return home, up-wind.

Consecutive drives should not be parallel, unless the drives are divided by a ridge which provides 'dead ground' for both drives. If the second parallel drive is in full view of the first, many birds will move out of the second drive, to the side, while the first is in progress.

Avoid driving grouse over wide, open valleys. The natural flight of grouse is along the contour. They prefer to swing round the end of a hill, returning to their home ground, rather than cross a wide valley to new ground. In very hilly country there are exceptions to this rule, where they may be driven over short distances from hill to hill, and of course they will fly over narrow ravines very readily.

Figure 3 (which shows the same area as Figure 1) illustrates a simple layout of butts suitable for any wind direction. Drives 2 and 4 are to a line of butts sited on fairly flat open ground. If the two 'hills' being driven were much higher and more widely separated, these drives would not work, as the birds would tend to swing round the ends of the hills. In such a situation the butts should be as shown in Figure 4. This will provide two parallel drives, but because the beaters doing one drive cannot be seen by birds on the other, there is no objection. I know one small, partly wooded hill of this shape which is driven in one drive. This drive produces grouse, blackgame and capercaillie, and they come from both directions, sometimes simultaneously. I know no more exciting drive anywhere in Britain.

Blackgame, another important game species to be found on moorland areas, are birds of the fringe of the moor, where moor-

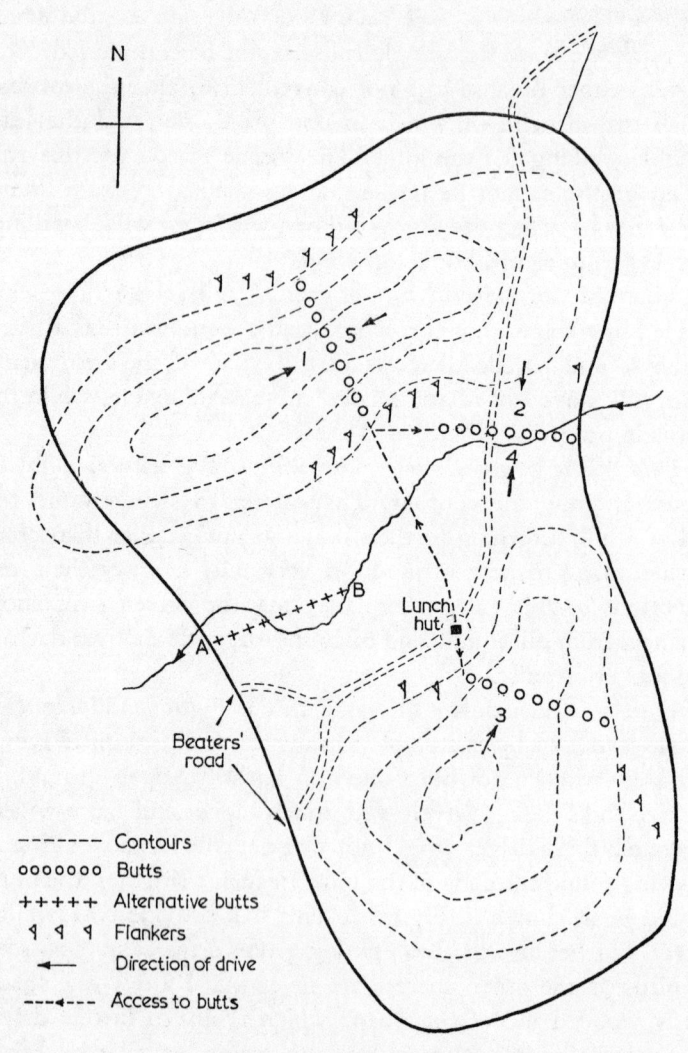

Fig 3 Butting a moor

Layout of butts for five drives with prevailing wind south-west (the same moor as shown in Fig 1). On a normal day, guns assemble at lunch hut and walk to drives 1, 2 and 3 before lunch, and to 4 and 5 after lunch. With these butts and the spare line A–B, a down-wind drive can always start the day.

36

```
P    Flankers
ooo  Butts
→    Direction of drive
```

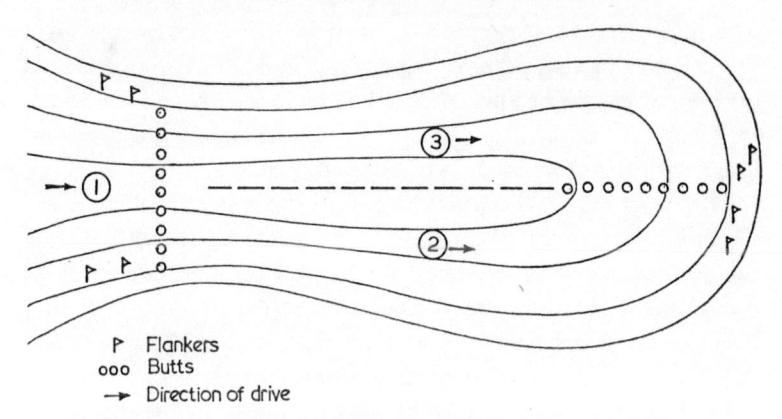

Fig 4   Siting butts on a spur

For drives 2 and 3 the beaters are divided, half taking drive 2, the others bringing in drive 3 afterwards.

land, conifer forest and oat fields meet. An old blackcock sailing over the guns on a fine October morning is a thrilling sight, as well as a fair test for the gun who is lucky enough to be underneath him. Blackgame fly faster than grouse, yet they are very deceptive, because they appear to be floating over slowly with slow wingbeats on oiled wings.

Blackgame come into season on 20 August and, with grouse, go out on 10 December. But early in the season old birds have not recovered from the moult and the young have not gained their full powers of flight. They may be found in heather, rushes, bracken and other places with reasonable cover, and at that time they sit tight and are flushed and shot easily.

When the mountain-ash berries are ripe, blackgame will be found in dingles or hedgerows in which these trees are growing. Like grouse, they are fond of bilberries, cranberries and all the other moorland berries. Unlike grouse, however, blackgame will eat heather beetles, which at times do so much harm to heather.

After mid-September it is unusual to be able to walk up blackgame. They will rise almost as soon as they see danger. Therefore little drives must be arranged. It is important for the guns to get into position without being seen, and they must be placed on the natural flight line, for blackgame cannot be driven where they have no wish to go. They fly great distances and a second drive with the same birds is not easy to arrange.

The question of whether to shoot greyhens is one which every organiser of a shoot must decide. Often it is accepted that only the blackcock should be shot, and where they are not numerous this is the right decision. But where they are plentiful, then I believe that some greyhens may be shot, as long as plenty are left. It is not very easy to shoot a high proportion of the stock.

Blackgame feed on oat stubbles, or stooks, frequently. They can be flighted on to the field in the morning or driven from the field over guns hidden on a suitable line of flight during the day. Where oat fields adjoin moorland, grouse will also use them, but blackgame will fly greater distances to stubbles. Sometimes they will lie in roots or potatoes.

Of course the most frequent habitat is woodland, especially young Scots pine, or lodge-pole pine. They feed on the buds of pine and so foresters dislike them, a little unreasonably as I believe, for the damage often appears worse than it is, and trees have a remarkable power of recovery. In 1939 I had under my charge Dyfnant forest, amongst others, near Lake Vyrnwy in Wales. There was a large heathery knoll planted with lodge-pole pine, and blackgame ate the bud out of every leading shoot. The war intervened and it was some twelve years before I was able to return. I sought out this heathery knoll. There was a solid crop of lodge-pole pine, which had killed out all the heather. There was no sign even of distortion to the boles of the trees near ground level, where the severe damage had occurred. Certainly there is no excuse whatsoever for foresters to destroy nests of blackgame. This is just as illegal as a man destroying trees and, anyway, the value of the sporting may well exceed the value of the timber crop, where this is of low quality through site conditions.

In the spring, blackgame gather together on a grassy knoll,

or open field, to lek. Leks are traditional places for courtship (like deer rutting stands), and will be used by many generations of blackgame. The cocks display before the greyhens, one cock usually being dominant. Mating takes place at the lek.

One June evening I was returning from a foray after roe, when I saw five blackcocks on a lek. There were no greyhens, as by then the hens were sitting on eggs. Eric Stevens and I sat in his Range Rover to watch these cocks strutting up and down and listened to their very beautiful love call, which has a wild haunting music: a sort of 'roc cooing', which carries a very long way. There was a hen whinchat on a gorse bush beside the lek and a pair of short-eared owls sweeping on silent wings to and fro over the area.

Suddenly, about a hundred yards away, we saw a cock capercaillie. He was about a mile from the nearest caper wood. He spread his tail, and with drooping wings and tiny mincing steps he set a course straight for the lek. He moved very smoothly and quite quickly, as if he was on wheels, until he swept regally on to the middle of the lek, where he proceeded to march up and down, glorious in his splendour. The blackcocks were very put out. Now silent, their lyre-shaped tails drooping, they slunk off to the side of the lek, where they remained hidden. The whole incident was fascinating and one that must be exceedingly rare to witness. What a pity there were no greyhens present!

The caper, or capercaillie, is the last of the grouse family to be found in Britain, reintroduced in the last century, but he cannot be claimed to be really a bird of the rough shoot. He is a magnificent bird, regal, almost fearsome in appearance, as he has a baleful eye and great neck hackles like those of an eagle and a very strong, evil-looking beak. He is the fastest game bird of all, and will fly with incredible speed, as straight as an arrow, right through a tree crop. How he avoids flying into a branch is a mystery.

I had a very large black labrador retriever named Bear. Once, after he had retrieved a cock caper which I had shot, I made him lie down, and then I marked the point of his nose and the root of his tail with small stones. After this I laid the cock caper with his beak on one stone. His tail was two inches beyond the other. (A repeat experiment with Bear on my sitting-room carpet made that 42½in.) A cock caper will weigh 12lb. The hen is much smaller with beautiful fawn and buff markings.

Caper should always be driven. Even then they fly low on most occasions, although I have seen them come high over a deep ravine, where they looked no bigger than grouse—clean out of shot. There is no greater achievement with a shotgun than a right and left at cock caper. I have seen it done once, when Eric killed a right and left at cocks, a right and left at hens, and a single bird, at the first stand at his first caper shoot. He will never do that again, for one is lucky to get two or three shots in a day's driving.

Caper became extinct around 1750 and they were reintroduced in 1837 in Perthshire. They are very difficult to hand-rear, even with partridge crumbs. Foresters dislike them as they eat pine and larch shoots, so it is praiseworthy that an attempt was made in 1970 to introduce them to the Lake District. However, it is not certain that this was successful and it may be that the rainfall is on the high side. Apart from that, they occur only in Scottish forests, mainly in the Highlands. They require a good proportion of middle-aged or mature pine, and truly they are the 'cock of the woods'.

There are two British forests which I consider to be ideally suited to caper—Clocaenog forest in North Wales and Thetford Chase in East Anglia. Let us hope that one day they will be introduced to both areas.

Most people consider the flesh to be tainted with resin, but I have eaten many caper and I have never had one which was unpleasant. The secret is to clean out the crop with meticulous care and to cook them in a very slow oven. Blackgame are sometimes tainted, too, but they have three-coloured flesh on the breast, a small part being pink like salmon, a wider strip being white like a French partridge, and the rest being grouse-coloured.

The open season for caper is 1 October to 31 January. Hens should be shot very sparingly—say one hen only to each gun per day.

I have dealt with the subject of moor management at some length because it is a very specialised subject, and the man who takes a rough moorland shoot cannot be expected to have the same specialised knowledge as the man who owns a first-class moor.

Yet the improvement of a rough moorland shoot is so very well worthwhile, apart from the fact that it will give great pleasure. It takes time and energy, but there are no costly rearing expenses—and grouse are magnificent sporting birds.

4
The Low Ground Shoot: Partridge, Pheasant, Woodcock

As far as game is concerned, there is no doubt that the mainstay of the low ground (in contrast to moorland) is the pheasant. This is a major change in the countryside, since the days of my youth, when the partridge was the chief game species of the small shoot. How well I remember the happy September days when my father and I, with our dogs, accompanied by a single beater, used to shoot partridges together on small farms in Shropshire. They were made up of small fields and the farming practice in those days was dependent upon a rotation of crops. Each field might hold a covey and the whole day's shooting required a high degree of fieldcraft and a sound knowledge of every part of the area and, particularly, a very good insight into the detailed behaviour and habits of partridges. Today I doubt if one would find one covey on the entire area that we used to cover in a whole day. Just as the partridges have gone—largely owing to the modern methods of farming: large fields with poor nesting cover, crop spraying, silage and, in many areas, the continued cropping of the same fields with the same crop, especially in barley-growing areas—so too has the knowledge of partridge habits and behaviour deteriorated.

I have heard the host say: 'Let us walk the roots first. There's a covey of partridges about somewhere and they are sure to be there.' What nonsense! A generation ago no one would have thought of such folly.

Early in the day partridges will be found on the open ground: grass fields, stubbles, even bare fallow, but not in roots. As the ground warms up, they will work their way to thick cover—potatoes, root fields, or, where there are no such crops, to rough pasture with rushes or other natural cover. How well they used to love the wild fields of scabious, thyme and rough grass! How rare such fields are today.

In wet weather they might go into a thin crop of potatoes, but they would avoid root crops. If they were put in, it would not be long before they would be out again. Common turnips ('neeps' in Scotland) are slightly preferred in wet weather to swedes ('sweds'), and kale provides better cover than these or mangolds or sugar beet, even when wet. In a wet autumn partridges may not learn to use roots at all.

However, in hot, dry weather, the middle part of the day will be spent in the shade of root crops.

In wild, stormy weather partridges will be hard to find, as they shelter in odd corners and close under hedgerows, sometimes even inside a wide straggling hedge.

In the middle to late afternoon, they will return to the open fields, stubbles, pasture, etc. Alas, in these days, stubbles are cut close and they are ploughed in almost as soon as the harvest is off—another adverse factor for the partridge. So too is the unpleasant practice of burning the straw, which has nothing to commend it from the point of view of game or other wildlife.

When walking up partridges on the rough shoot, the foregoing basic facts must be borne in mind. Start on the open ground, stubbles and fields, and work the birds always towards cover. Do not leave out any ground because you do not think they'll be there. Above all, do not cut corners. So often the birds will creep ahead of the guns and end up in a corner of the field. If the outside gun cuts the corner, they will not be flushed. That is why the outside gun, if he covers the ground properly, often gets most of the shooting.

When birds have been flushed and put into cover, a decision must be made as to whether to follow up at once, or leave them until later, when all the outside fields have been worked into the roots. If it is a damp day, follow them at once. If it is warm and dry, they may be left for an hour or so—but not if they are put in late in the day.

In wild weather, or late in the season, partridges will not lie well. They will tend to rise out of shot. That is when a very detailed knowledge of the habits and whereabouts of each covey is necessary. An impromptu drive or two should be arranged, because if the big covey of eighteen can be put over the guns they will tend to split up, and the shock of being saluted from in front will cause them to lie better afterwards, when a bag may be made.

When there are sufficient partridges to have a full driving day, which will not be the case very often on a rough shoot, the precise placing of the guns is of vital importance. They should be placed behind a tall hedge, not too close, but also not too far behind. It is critical to get the exact position, so that each gun can take the leading birds as they top the hedge, thus splitting the covey to the two guns on each side of him. Ideally the field of cover (roots, etc) to which the birds are driven should be about 400yd behind the guns. When this field is driven in turn, the birds will tend to come out in ones and twos because they have been split up, and a good bag will result.

What can be done to encourage partridges? The key lies in farming practice, and unless the farmer is a member of the shoot it is difficult to bring about even a small degree of alteration to farming practice in order to aid them. One can improve the nesting cover a little here and there by planting gorse or broom in clumps along wire fences. Electric pylons are useful for this, because a length of sheep netting can be put round the four uprights and gorse and broom planted within, secure from grazing animals.

One adverse factor is the intense cultivation of every yard of ground. In June, when partridges hatch, there is very little open ground where the young birds can go to dry out and dust, if wet. On a rainy day in June the whole farm is a sea of wet vegetation. If a few yards can be left fallow on the south (sunny) side of hedges, that will prove to be a great advantage.

THE LOW GROUND SHOOT: PARTRIDGE, PHEASANT, WOODCOCK

During the lean months of the year (January to April) modern farms present a barren, bleak wilderness with the minimum of cover. Narrow strips of rape sown immediately after harvest and left until the spring ploughing and sowing will provide invaluable winter cover. Here partridges may be fed. Successful breeding of all game birds, and wildfowl, depends upon the parent birds reaching the nesting time in good health and condition. Winter feed helps them to achieve this and ensures fertile eggs and healthy chicks. Better than rape are strips of kale which are left right through to the spring. Such patches of kale will also increase the bag of pheasants enormously.

It is easy to hand-rear partridges nowadays. But rearing on a large scale has not proved very successful. They tend to pack early and disappear quickly. However, on the rough shoot, rearing a covey or two under bantams, at widely spaced distances, may help to recolonise partridges in areas from which they have died out.

Perhaps the most important factor of all in the partridge world is Ascot week! If the ladies' hats and dresses are ruined by rain, there will be no partridges—because that is the week when they hatch, and day-old chicks will snuff out like candles in a wind, once they get really wet and bedraggled.

As partridge hatching time is wet so very often the pheasant is the mainstay of game on the rough shoot.

Modern methods of rearing pheasants are relatively simple, and the Game Conservancy publication Booklet No 8, *Pheasant Rearing*, gives detailed directions, so I do not intend to elaborate on rearing. But however small the rough shoot may be, it should be possible to increase the stock of pheasants by rearing a few, even if this is done only on the lawn. Perhaps the most simple method is to buy in day-old chicks and rear them in a brooder.

It is not always realised that the crucial time, when the highest mortality may occur, is the time of establishing them in the release pen, and thence into the natural or wild habitat. Of course, it is a complete waste of time to rear any if the habitat is unsuitable, or if the whole shoot is crawling with vermin.

THE LOW GROUND SHOOT: PARTRIDGE, PHEASANT, WOODCOCK

Lucky is he who is the owner of a rough shoot, for then he can carry out many improvements over the years, which will bring him much pleasure and enhance his sport greatly.

A shooting tenant cannot be expected to plant new plantations. However, if he has a long lease (and it is desirable that all shoots should be held on as long a lease as possible to give security of tenure) there is much that can be done to improve the shoot for pheasants, provided the owner and his farming tenant are agreeable.

The most important single item that needs to be improved on nearly every rough shoot for pheasants is 'holding cover'—trees, shrubs and bushes, which will provide warmth and shelter, and also make holding ground from which to flush birds. (At the other extreme are the large areas of young plantations, in the thicket stage, such as are many of the Forestry Commission forests. Here there is too much dense cover, too little open ground for sunning and dusting, and a low proportion of natural feed.)

Very often there is a small stream with alders and scrub, or corners on dry banks with gorse, blackthorn, broom, etc. Where such places are open to grazing, there will be no cover. But if permission can be obtained to fence out the stock, then the scrub will soon grow thick and make cover for nesting, and also for holding pheasants, and the odd woodcock, in winter.

Let us therefore assume that we have a free hand to do anything we wish, which is the owner's position: at least it is if he farms the land himself. How much can be done must be decided in each separate instance, but it is very rare that nothing at all can be done, provided the members of the shoot are active and keen enough to put in some hard work. Here it should be remembered that sporting rents are high. They are likely to increase. Anything which can be done to improve the sporting value is an asset to the estate.

Basically there are two lines on which to work: first, to improve existing conditions, and second, to provide new habitats.

When improving existing conditions one must work with what

is already on the ground. As has been said, a lot can be done to encourage natural cover by fencing out stock. The existing woodland will need attention, too. Many plantations are of conifers only. During the thicket stage they are too thick, but by brashing, or cutting off the lower branches of one side of two adjoining rows, access for beaters can be provided—or for three or four guns to walk through with their dogs. Positions for forward guns may need clearing and opening up, so that a clear shot may be obtained.

The next stage in a conifer plantation is the reverse of the thicket stage, as the dense foliage during that period will kill off all ground cover. The floor of the plantation will become bare and draughty, with neither food nor shelter. If sylvicultural thinnings are delayed too long that will make matters worse. Therefore it is desirable to thin as early as is practical. Ideally some groups of trees should be thinned extra heavily so as to encourage some ground vegetation to come in, as this is dependent upon light. These groups should be chosen with careful forethought, so that they can be developed into flushing-points as the woodland develops. Indeed, as soon as enough light has been admitted, some planting of species suitable to provide ground cover should be done. Preference should be given to those shrubs known to do well in the locality. Laurel is a useful species as are *Lonicera nitida, Galtheria, Cotoneaster microphylla* and many other species. An excellent arrangement is to fell enough of the initial crop to make room for groups of Norway spruce to be planted. These groups can be managed on a Christmas-tree basis, thus providing some return and, if replanted at intervals, permanent flushing-points. Another sound practice is to underplant the heavily thinned groups with western hemlock (*Tsuga*). This tree will persist under quite heavy shade and gradually form a second storey.

Attention should be paid to the outer edges of draughty plantations. If there was a hedge originally, some felling of overhead trees coupled with careful trimming will help to thicken it up. If the tree crop has thick branches down to ground level, these branches should be retained. But if the outer edge is thin and open, it is desirable to thicken it up by planting shrub or hedge species. This may be necessary only on the most exposed side of the wood.

When it comes to creating entirely new habitats, there is a very much greater choice of action. It may be only a case of making use of a waste bank, or corner, where it is not worthwhile to plant up with a timber crop. A dry south bank (which is always favoured by pheasants) is suitable for broom, a natural species which makes excellent game cover. It is easy to collect the seed from the natural pods in August, as soon as they turn black. Before sowing in spring, the seed should have boiling water poured on to it and then it should be left overnight to soak. This will hasten germination. Broom can also be propagated from cuttings taken in July by anyone who has the enthusiasm to give the necessary attention to this method.

On dry, sandy soil two species which are easy to establish are tree lupin (from seed) and sea buckthorn (from cuttings or slips of root). Both make excellent game cover. Juniper is another very useful species on chalk soils and on many sites in Scotland.

Waste corners of wet ground can be made to produce ground cover by planting unrooted shoots of sallow (*Salix caprea* and others) in March. All these things can be done by one or two enthusiasts on the rough shoot.

The forming of new plantations is a matter for the owner. In hill country, which is the most usual source of rough shooting, there are many places which have large areas of bracken. This type of ground is excellent for conversion into pheasant coverts. The ideal size is about ten acres, with twenty acres being quite enough for one block.

What trees should be grown? Here the forester must make some allowance for game requirements, just as the shooting fanatic should concede that the operation must provide the estate with a woodland income. It is a very clever man who can forecast the financial return from any plantation, and most of those

Page 49 (*above*) Decide first in what part of the country you want to live; (*below*) heather-burning

Page 50 (*above*) Two guns starting out; (*below*) most shoots have the odd small pond

THE LOW GROUND SHOOT: PARTRIDGE, PHEASANT, WOODCOCK

who attempt this exercise confuse the issue by a complexity of erudite formulae which may or may not bear some relation to the true position sixty years forward. So, let us be content to look at the basic facts relating to a few of those tree species which may be used. It should not be forgotten that the Forestry Commission will give excellent expert advice as to what species will grow upon any given site, and the address of the nearest office will be found in the local telephone directory.

The ideal pheasant covert should contain a mixture of conifers (mainly evergreens) for roosting, and of hardwoods (mainly broad-leaved trees), particularly those which provide food such as acorns, beech mast and certain berries. There are three larches —European, Japanese and the hybrid. European is fussy in its site requirements. Japanese is easy. But hybrid larch combines the best qualities of both and is recommended. Commercially it is not a heavy volume producer, but it is a useful estate tree for posts, rails and so on. It is fast-growing in its early stages and it will make cover for game quickly. In the thicket stage it forms an ideal habitat for woodcock. In middle and later ages it can be opened up and underplanted. Therefore it is a very useful tree for planting in large groups in pheasant coverts.

Douglas fir is a large volume producer and valuable timber tree on good loams and brown earths where exposure is not severe. It is a useful game covert species. Even better is western hemlock, also a great volume producer and not very exacting except as to severe exposure. It withstands considerable shade and will regenerate freely.

Of the spruces, sitka spruce withstands extreme exposure on sites which are far too exposed for pheasants and will produce a very large volume of timber on acid soils in high-rainfall areas. But any of the other conifers is preferable for pheasants, because sitka spruce is so prickly—bad also for beaters. Norway spruce is slower-growing. Except for heather ground and severe exposure, where it should not be used, its requirements are broadly similar to those of sitka. Both will grow better than other conifers on wet ground, after suitable draining. It is a useful tree for flushing-points, where it can be managed on a Christmas-tree rotation.

Three pines may be considered for heathland conditions. Corsican pine is the largest volume producer, but it is not suitable for high rainfall, high elevations or the northern climate. Scots pine is a very low volume producer, but it grows fast and makes cover in the early stages. Far too much use of this species has been made to plant up good grouse moors, with the ultimate possibility of growing low-quality timber, very slowly! Lodgepole pine (*Pinus contorta*) is the most tolerant tree of all for really poor conditions. It is very quick-growing, but it is a low volume producer of low value. It too has been used to ruin many good grouse moors, where it will be vulnerable to damage by deer (bark stripping) throughout most of its rotation. However, it has a use for making cover quickly for pheasants.

None of the other conifers need be considered. None of the hardwoods is likely to produce a very economic crop, so we can consider them on their merits for game only. Beech, which provides valuable mast for pheasant feed, is a relatively difficult species to establish because it is prone to damage by frost, mouse, rabbit, hare, squirrel and deer for a long period. Let it be used where it is known to succeed well: on calcareous soils. Ash is not a very good game tree, except that its foliage is light and therefore it encourages good ground cover. It needs base-rich soils. Oak for commercial timber should be confined to the best soils, ie the wheat-growing soils. But Turkey oak, commercially a valueless species, is not at all exacting. It will grow well on poor soil and produce acorns at a relatively early stage. It should be considered. Red oak is a quick-growing, lovely species for reasonably good sites.

If they can be obtained, the two Chile beeches are excellent hardwoods, fast-growing and very productive of mast readily eaten by pheasants. *Nothofagus procera* is suitable for the wetter hill country and *N. obliqua* for lower rainfall areas in the south and east.

For wet areas, poplars (*Poplar trichocarpa* × *P. tachomahaka* clone

32 being recommended) and alders (*Alnus cordata* being the fastest growing) are suitable. Poplars, particularly, are ideal for planting in front of gun stands in order to make birds fly well. In fifteen to twenty years this object will be achieved—faster than with any other species except perhaps *A. cordata*.

Birch is a graceful tree worthy of retention if it occurs naturally. It is short-lived and therefore not worth planting especially. Sycamore and the maples are very prone to squirrel damage. They also cast dense shade and their only merit for pheasant covers is their ability to withstand exposure. Sweet chestnut is a useful species and it is ideal for management on a coppice basis.

Some of the smaller trees should be considered. Cherry (gean) is a beautiful species for amenity. Its relative, bird cherry (*Prunus padus*), is excellent for hill country where it will tolerate wet, acid conditions and quite a lot of exposure. Stransvesia is an excellent small tree which bears profuse red berries ripe at Christmas when they are most needed. *Cotoneaster frigidus* is somewhat similar, as its red berries ripen at Christmas. Snowy mespilus (*Amelanchier canadensis*) is a very beautiful species with snowy white flowers and good autumn foliage, which will be propagated by birds eating the berries. The mountain ash is too well known to describe. Its berries ripen in late August and early September, which is before they are needed. However, it is sought by blackgame where they are present.

The ideal pheasant cover will be a mixture of some of the aforementioned species chosen with a view to providing cover, protection from wind, roosting trees, variety (hardwoods), winter food (berried species and acorn or mast trees) and perhaps just beauty.

It must not be overlooked that a lot can be done to improve conditions for pheasants by bending the farming practice. It is most useful to grow patches of special game mixture which has no agricultural value, or artichokes, or buckwheat. But the most important thing to do is to grow patches of kale, especially in areas where the normal farming methods provide no crop cover and where pheasant woodlands are few and far between.

It will be necessary to come to some financial arrangement

with the farmer for growing kale, which may be costly, but there is no doubt at all that in most cases it will pay handsomely to halve the cost of the rearing and to spend the money thus saved on growing kale. The bag at the end of the season will be greater. Where possible it is desirable to keep some kale right through to March for shelter. This is even more important for partridges.

Even on a rough shoot it is very desirable to feed pheasants at suitable places. A suitable place is not necessarily where you want the pheasants to be. First of all it must be a good natural habitat for them—ie where *they* want to be.

There is one thing that is just as important as feeding. That is the human voice. If your guns are prone to coffee-housing, calling out to each other, shouting at their dogs, their wives or their children, or even talking to themselves, you may as well save the cost of rearing or feeding, as both will prove to be a waste of money. The human voice travels a long way. A cock pheasant will travel farther, very quickly.

Even on a rough shoot, the judicious placing of 'stops', who may be children, provided they are carefully instructed and placed, will add to the bag considerably. Of course, it is essential that all guns should know exactly where the stops are placed.

The question of the various breeds of pheasants must be considered—Mongolian ring-neck, old English black neck, Chinese, Melanistic and Japanese. One hears it said: 'I tried some Melanistic last year, but they were seen to wander everywhere.' Any race which is distinctive enough to be recognised easily, as is the dark green Melanistic cock (with dark brown grouse-like hens), and which is numerically fewer than other races present, will appear to wander more than the others. I doubt whether there is any significant difference between the wandering habits of the various races. They all wander. The Japanese is a possible exception. I don't think enough is known of it yet. The Chinese is a most beautiful race, but it is possible that it is more prone to predation than the others, simply because, being paler, it shows up more easily.

The Japanese pheasant is the least well known. It is very attractive and considerably smaller than the other races. The cock is green with blue shoulders. The hen reminds me a little of the reeves hen, but she is much smaller. They come from a high-rainfall region and it is reasonable to suppose that they will succeed better than the common pheasant in high-rainfall hill country in Britain. But I do not think that this has been proved to be the case without any shadow of doubt, although I know of one instance when Japanese chicks survived a wet period better than ordinary chicks, all in similar rearing pens on the same site. One difficulty is that they interbreed with ordinary pheasants, so that it is not easy to maintain a pure feral race. Nor is it easy to find an area where there are no ordinary pheasants at all, except where conditions are too severe for survival anyway. All one can say is that they show some promise for the rough shoot where conditions, owing to high rainfall, are poor.

Of the ornamental pheasants, reeves is the only one which flies well. The tail of the cock is 5ft long, which aids it considerably when it comes high over the guns. But it is a very pugnacious bird amongst other pheasants. Golden and lady amherst are very beautiful birds, but they skulk in thick cover and fly only a few feet from the ground. They are also pugnacious. Whilst goldens are established in many areas in a feral state, pure amhersts are not frequently found because the two species interbreed and the so-called feral amhersts (as in the New Forest) carry golden blood. The cocks have the silver 'cape' or hackles of the amherst, but they also have red feathers on the flanks—a sure sign of golden influence. None of these breeds is of significance for the rough shoot, or as sporting birds.

The most exciting bird of the low ground is the woodcock. It is the special prize of the rough shoot, and more woodcock are missed through over-excitement than from any other cause.

The open season is from 1 September to 31 January in Scotland, and from 1 October to 31 January in England and Wales. There appears to me to be no logical reason for this difference, but there it is.

THE LOW GROUND SHOOT: PARTRIDGE, PHEASANT, WOODCOCK

Many woodcock breed in Britain where their leisurely roding flight in spring, accompanied by a strange croaking grunt (and sometimes a squeak which I, for one, cannot hear) is one of the pleasant sights of the British woodland scene. How often, when stalking a roe buck in spring, one sees this special courting flight. It is one of nature's regular events to which I look forward every year. They nest early, in March, laying four comparatively large eggs. The parent bird (I cannot say whether only the female or both sexes) will carry its young, when threatened by danger, to another area of the forest. This is well recorded and I have witnessed it on four occasions. On two of these occasions the young bird was almost fully fledged. The young is carried between the thighs, with its legs dangling.

Most of these home-bred birds seem to move off in the autumn, probably migrating to Spain and North Africa. Their place is taken by woodcock coming across the North Sea from northern Europe and it is these birds which provide our sport, although, in the days when it was legal to shoot woodcock up to 1 March, it was mostly the home-bred birds, returning, which were available at that time.

Most bird migration is remarkably regular, year by year, and it is my experience that the main 'fall' of woodcock arrives with the first full moon of November. If there are adverse winds they will flop down as soon as they make landfall, and sometimes the dunes on the east coast are full of woodcock for a day or two. After that the main numbers move west. Favoured areas may be blessed by a 'fall' of woodcock almost anywhere in Britain. For one day they will be everywhere in a suitable habitat. Lucky the rough shooter who encounters a fall just once in a lifetime! Let him take full advantage there and then. If he invites his friends to shoot the next day, he will find that he is too late, as most of the woodcock will have disappeared. On rare occasions, just after dark, when returning from an outing after fallow deer, I have encountered many woodcock along the forest roads, lit by the car headlights. This indicates a sudden arrival. They will be gone the next day.

THE LOW GROUND SHOOT: PARTRIDGE, PHEASANT, WOODCOCK

Most shoots have a small resident winter population of woodcock, although the numbers fluctuate greatly and there are times when none seem to be present. Always they have their favoured areas and, provided the state of the tree crop or natural vegetation remains the same, woodcock will be found in the same places year after year. Sometimes a certain specific holly bush, or clump of gorse or whin, or patch of birch, will hold a woodcock every winter, and when the local occupant is shot, he will be replaced by another fairly quickly.

Woodcock feed at night and they flight, usually singly, at dusk and dawn, just as duck do, but usually a few minutes earlier at dusk. There are some places where a regular flight may be encountered. These places are usually between dry daytime cover and wet marshland. Woodcock feed on worms, so an acid peat bog, which holds no worms, is not good feeding ground. But wet mineral soil contains many worms and provides a favourite feeding habitat.

During hard weather and, to a lesser extent, during the dark of the moon, woodcock will be found by day feeding in woodland springs and beside small streams.

What is their favourite daytime cover? Dead bracken, Japanese or hybrid larch in the thicket stage before the forest floor becomes bare, young birches in the thicket stage, or old birch trees with dense bracken, broom banks, gorse when it is middle-aged to old, sometimes rhododendron, or laurels, or dark conifers (such as western hemlock) with branches sweeping the ground; and, of course, alders, chiefly because alders grow where there is often a spring or good moist feeding ground.

Every enthusiastic woodcock shooter should keep a special woodcock diary in which he should note the weather conditions, and the exact type of cover where woodcock have been found. This is sound advice. I wish I had done it myself! (Indeed, the same recommendation applies to all game or wildfowl—especially geese—and, of course, deer.)

Where I live there is a two-acre birch wood ideal for woodcock. But it holds a 'cock very rarely. However, at the side is a belt of fairly old gorse some 70yd long and 5yd wide. Under normal weather this does not hold woodcock either. But when there is an inch of snow, there are always up to three woodcock there. This is because an inch of snow with me means deep snow on the higher ground and the 'cock move down to my locality, where conditions are less severe. So a knowledge of precisely what conditions suit woodcock in each different locality is very necessary. One other requirement is freedom from disturbance. The woodcock is a lone ranger and he does not welcome intrusion upon his range. Many a good locality for woodcock has been deserted when a large number of pheasants has been reared. These vulgar birds spoil the privacy of the woodcock.

On a rough shoot the best way with woodcock is for two guns, who know the ground and each other well, to go out together with one or two good dogs. They should hunt the likely places, each gun on opposite sides. On steep ground they should work the contour, one above the other. Where there is a long ravine or wooded gully, one gun should go forward to a suitable vantage-point.

Woodcock are reputedly difficult to shoot. This is because, so often, they occur amongst trees and they are adept at disappearing behind a tree or bush. But in the open they present a very easy shot. They may appear to fly fast, but their speed is much less than that of a mallard, pheasant or grouse.

Many people think that woodcock do not run. In thick cover they do not do so often. But I have seen a woodcock run quite a long way in front of beaters, and a winged 'cock may run, where the ground is bare.

The legs of a woodcock (which are the greatest delicacy on the table) should be drawn immediately after the bird is shot, whilst it is warm. The 'pen feathers' are no longer sought after by artists, but they are often worn by the triumphant sportsman in his hat. He who obtains a right or left at woodcock, and can find two witnesses, qualifies for a bottle of Bols. The only two times I have brought off a right and left resulted in no Bols, because on the first occasion there was no witness and, on the other occasion, the second bird could not be found. It fell in dense gorse and I believe that it stuck in a thick gorse bush above the ground. Certainly a long search was ineffective.

In Britain the best areas for woodcock shooting are in Eire and Northern Ireland and also those parts of the west coast of England, Wales and Scotland which may be said to be collecting-points for the last-stage migration to Eire. Less certain, but sometimes very good, are the arrival points on the east coast.

The west coast areas may be defined in broad terms as Cornwall, west Pembrokeshire, the Lleyn peninsula in Caernarvon, parts of Anglesey to a lesser extent, some parts of Mull of Galloway, and Mull of Kintyre, Islay (particularly good), Mull, sometimes parts of Skye and some places in the Orkneys (eg Rousay). All these areas are predominantly bleak, and woodcock are found where there are suitable habitats such as the hazel woods of the Lleyn peninsula. No doubt careful planting would add to the good woodcock shoots in these areas.

The Conservation Section of the Wildfowlers Association of Great Britain and Ireland (WAGBI) has undertaken an intensive study of woodcock, and no doubt much more will be known about this delightful and exciting bird in a few years' time.

Marsh and Wildfowl

In practice, marshland is part of the low ground and usually it will merge with agricultural land on the one hand and woodland on the other, just as woodland will sometimes occur on the fringe of the moor. Partridges will be found on the marshes, and the pheasant is just as much a marshland bird as a woodland one. Both species are fond of jugging, or roosting, on marshland, often in very wet conditions. Grouse too, particularly old cocks, like to roost on very wet moorland bogs. I believe that this preference for roosting in wet places is because at night they can hear foxes (or men) splashing through the water. When partridges jug they form a very tight circle, heads facing outwards. Pheasants jug separately. However, this chapter is about wildfowl rather than game birds. But it must not be forgotten that marshland is very good holding ground, and both pheasants and partridges can be moved very easily from bare stubbles and pasture into the marsh. When marshes contain *Phragmites* reeds (the 'Norfolk reed' used for thatching), the reed bed is a hazard because it is almost impossible to drive pheasants out again. A reed bed becomes a sanctuary for pheasants and it is of very little use for the shooter.

Roe deer (and sika too, where they are present) love reed beds. They also occur on marshland even at considerable distances from woodland. Many years ago I visited the Neusiedler Sea in Austria near the Hungarian border. It is one of the most spectacular inland waters, for a huge variety of waterfowl occur there, from glossy ibis to bean goose. Unfortunately, when I was there it was frozen so hard that one could have driven a car over it. The only birds we saw were two greylags and a rough-legged buzzard. But in the evening many roe came out of the fringe of tall reeds to feed on the highly cultivated land adjoining. The reed beds also held a fair stock of wild boar.

In Scotland anyone who arrives in Inverness by the night train, during a time of year when it is light enough to see, can hardly fail to spot a roe or two on the large expanse of marshland beside the Spey, between Newtonmore and Aviemore. There are times when floods sweep right across this area, but presumably the roe deer know where they will find safe ground. Anyway, they can swim perfectly well.

The main quarry species to be found on the marshes are snipe and ducks, the most frequently found being mallard, teal and wigeon. A small proportion of inland marshes will be used by geese, and where this is so, it is a great bonus for the rough shoot. However, it can be a disadvantage, because there will be many occasions when a conflict arises between the need to keep the area undisturbed for the sake of the geese, and the desire to take a fair toll of the other game which occupies the area. One way to get over this difficulty is to flight the geese at first light and then shoot game and snipe afterwards. But that is a compromise which is not satisfactory on all occasions, because one wants a full-scale gale for shooting geese and a calm, still day for game. Also, sport will last longer if one follows these pursuits on separate occasions rather than cram everything into one concentrated day.

Let us consider the geese first. One or more of four species may be encountered: greylags, pinkfeet, whitefronts and canadas.

Canadas are resident in Britain, where they have lost their migratory habits to a large extent. The notable exception is an interesting case, for the immature canada geese (ie birds one or two years old) of central Yorkshire, with adults that have lost their nests, migrate to the Beauly Firth in Inverness-shire in June each year for the annual moult, when all geese are flightless. They return in August, or sometimes as late as early September. Elsewhere, canadas in Britain assemble for the moult on one particular lake in each area, which is large enough for them to feel safe when flightless and which has ample grazing within easy walking distance. On the Beauly Firth, a tidal area, they feed on the saltings and also on *enteromorpha*—a green algal growth—and on *zostera*, both these species being the main winter food of brent geese.

However, this is a digression. Canada geese are fairly local in their movements, and as they are much less wild than the true wild geese, it is not difficult to ascertain their local movements and to flight them *en route* for feeding or roosting grounds. They also do not fly very high as a rule. They do fly fast and they are easy to miss on that account, because they appear to be moving slowly. They weigh up to 12lb and, if cooked very slowly, they are excellent to eat.

Grey geese roost on estuaries or large areas of inland water, flighting to the roost at dusk, or sometimes well before dusk. In the mornings they flight from the roost to their feeding grounds—stubbles or pasture in the early part of the season; after mid-November, potato fields, but not until those potatoes left from the harvest have been frosted; pastures and winter wheat from Christmas onwards. Whitefronted geese feed more on pastures than do pinkfeet and greylags. Greylags may use turnip fields during heavy snow.

Except for this last habit, which is a recent development, canadas (which are black geese) conform to this general behaviour, although they sometimes flight to feed in the evenings, like ducks. All geese may flight to their feeding grounds when there is a full moon, greylags doing this less frequently than the other species. But greylags are very likely to swim in to the edge of the roosting area, if suitable food is there, when the moon is full.

The time of flighting depends to some extent on the pressure of shooting. When there is but little shooting, they may flight in the half-light. When pressure is heavy, they flight to the fields in full daylight, and return in a good light, so they stand a better chance of seeing hidden gunners.

With these general facts in mind, one can make a plan to outwit them. If one's shoot lies within a general goose area and geese start using the marsh (or fields), they will 'build up' to large numbers quite quickly if undisturbed. Indeed, in such areas they will tend to use the same fields at about the same time of year, year after year. That gives one time to make some preparations in the off season. A large thick hide, such as one might use for pigeons, is of use only if it is located in dense natural cover. Elsewhere it is marvellous—except that geese will not come near it! A goose hide must blend perfectly with the surroundings, and, as the natural vegetation surrounding goose feeding ground is minimal, so too the hide must be minimal: best of all is a lying hide, as that needs the least cover. It is not difficult to shoot from a lying position; indeed, it is easy, because one is relaxed until the moment to shoot arrives. Then, when the geese are well within range, one sits up and takes first the farthest of the two chosen, then the nearer one which by then will be about the same distance as the first had been. The only snag is that one is confined to a narrow angle on the right (shooting from the right shoulder) and only about from seven o'clock to twelve o'clock on the left. Any bird flying behind one is perfectly safe.

A very good type of hide is a sunken butt, turfed, and similar to a grouse butt. But in marshland this is liable to flood. Therefore, a sunken tub is better. It should have a plastic bucket for baling out and a stout lid to keep off cattle.

Good decoys will make goose shooting easier. But that can lead to greediness. Let each person set a personal limit when shooting over decoys, somewhere between three and ten. More than that and the shoot becomes a shameful slaughter, for it is easy to shoot forty or more geese if they are decoying properly.

If one's shoot is not used by geese normally, and they start using it, then one must consider the position very carefully. If it is a chance visitation, then an immediate drive may result in success, remembering that the one beater, the geese and the guns must be in a straight line, the guns being on the natural flight line. But if the area is very suitable for geese, it may pay not to shoot them at all the first year. There is a fluctuating population of geese in many areas, and if some find peace and good food, others will join them. Gradually, or even quickly, a build-up of geese will take place until they are firmly established year after year.

Geese are wary birds, they fly high by nature, they are keen-sighted and very tough, but they are not gifted with super-cunning as some would have us believe. Nor is the picturesque story that they post a sentry, true. When feeding, each goose in turn puts up its head to look for danger, the old geese more frequently than the young: therefore there is always an 'umbrella head' on the lookout. Watch carefully and you will see that it is not the same bird all the time, although if an old gander becomes suspicious his head will remain alert for a long time. The myth that the sentry taps another on the shoulder to make him take over is explained by the fact that an old goose likes plenty of elbow-room when feeding: if another comes too near he will run at him, neck outstretched, to peck him if possible. The other goose, disturbed and alarmed, puts his head up and is then assumed to be the next sentry. Nor is it true that a scout is sent out early to look over the feeding grounds for danger. It is very often the case that a single goose does 'scout round' before the arrival of the main body of geese. These early geese are birds which have lost a mate, or young birds separated from the family party, or, exceptionally, pricked birds. Except for pricked birds, which more frequently arrive after the main body, these early geese call incessantly because they are seeking other geese—not wildfowlers!

The open season for geese and ducks is from 1 September to 31 January inland and to 20 February on tidal areas. The duck season used to open on 1 August. In Belgium it opens on 14 July, which is much too early. In Germany the season opens on 15 August. I see no reason at all why our open season should not be 15 August too (or even 12 August to match the opening date for grouse and snipe). As it is, the ducks which breed on moorland must not be shot with the grouse, and by the legal date most of them have moved. Some do get shot. I have seen a well-known judge kill a tall mallard very smartly, when it came over the butts on the Twelfth! In some areas many hundreds of mallard 'attack' barley and wheat fields just before harvest and they do heavy damage. They get shot in large numbers and no prosecutions follow, because a defence of 'preventing damage' would be likely to succeed. I have permission to shoot ducks on a farm which is on a very good flight line and where many flight to the barley. But by 1 September when I go they have all been shot up. As Jorrocks said, 'the law is an ass'. Perhaps one day there will be an international European opening date. If so, it is not likely to be as late as 1 September.

There are very few rough shoots which are not visited at some time or another by mallard. The habits of wild duck are the opposite to those of geese. Duck feed at night and rest during the day. Therefore they are flighting to their feeding ground at dusk and returning to their day resting-places—large sheets of water—at dawn. Exceptionally, when food is extra attractive, they cannot resist it during the day. Laid corn may attract mallard at dawn, or even odd ducks during the day: a fresh flood will draw them, and a thaw after a long hard spell will cause them to feed all day.

Because, normally, they feed at night, their presence may be unsuspected. They will have left long before the shooting party arrives. If there are large pools, lochs or lakes (ie daytime habitats), some knowledge of duck movements can be obtained in the off season. These areas will provide morning flighting. Butts should be put up in good time at suitable vantage-points. If the lake holds many ducks, it may be desirable to make a butt or two in the water—on piles if shallow, or on artificial islands if deep, or of course on existing islands. The butts must be occupied before first light, and a rough morning is ideal. If the lake is near the coastline, then morning flight should coincide with a rising tide, as a rough gale will move the ducks from the tideway to the shelter of the lake. The lake should not be shot more than once in three weeks. If ducks are visiting laid barley or wheat, droppings and the odd feather will be found. An evening or two spent watching and listening will soon give one an idea of how many ducks are coming and where they are feeding.

Most shoots have the occasional small pond, with a pair of moorhens, and such ponds are sometimes visited by mallard. If these ponds are fed (provided they are shallow enough) a regular flight will develop. Wheat, barley, potatoes make suitable feed. Many marshland areas have been drained, but, even so, in winter after heavy rainfall, shallow flashes of flood-water appear. These are visited by ducks at night. The odd feather will give an indication of the number coming. If the flash remains for some time, feed it first and then flight it. But if it **is** only a flash of short duration, then flight it at once. Very stale flood-water is not attractive to ducks.

Nearly every shoot has a small burn or stream running through it. In hard weather ducks will visit it and also any ditches which remain unfrozen. Large streams and rivers will have a regular daytime duck population. Then it will be found that there are favourite reaches, often with a mudbank or shingle bar where they rest. Backwaters are favoured particularly. Some ducks may be shot by arranging daytime drives from such places. But it is important to know the natural flight lines intimately, and for the standing guns to get in position stealthily—without firing at a tempting pigeon on the way. It is no use sitting on a shooting-stick in the open. The guns must be reasonably well concealed. Even so, not many ducks will be shot unless the weather is very rough. After the first flush the rest come over out of shot. It is far more productive to do the morning flight, placing a gun near each resting-place, to intercept them as they come in at dawn.

Picking-up is difficult. A dog sent at once for each duck shot may deter others from coming within shot. A picker-up, with two good dogs, should be stationed well down-stream of the lowest gun. Where many ducks are anticipated it is sound practice to stretch a net across the river. On a very wide river the picker-up should be in a boat, armed with a large landing-net.

Page 67 A high cock pheasant

Page 68 (*above*) Grouse behaviour; (*below*) roe kid

Each gun should note the number of 'wingers' and, if possible, despatch them with another shot, and in any case note as carefully as possible where they have gone, for hunting with a good dog later. And to those who say: 'All mine are killed stone dead', I would reply: 'How lucky—but I know miracles do happen'! Of course everything one shoots *should* be killed stone dead. Only the other day I heard of someone who killed forty-nine pigeons with forty-nine shots—and then ruined his whole day by using two cartridges on the last one. Well, marvellous! But we cannot all do that. If I was such a perfectionist, it would worry me so much when I missed that I would give up shooting.

What constitutes good shooting? It used to be said that if one takes all reasonable chances, at all species of game and 'fowl, one does well to average, thoughout the season, one kill for three cartridges. Many people shoot much better than that. But counting cartridges for kills leads to selfish and greedy shooting. Some guns are very adept at picking other people's birds. I have even known a gun with a reputation to keep up collect some of his

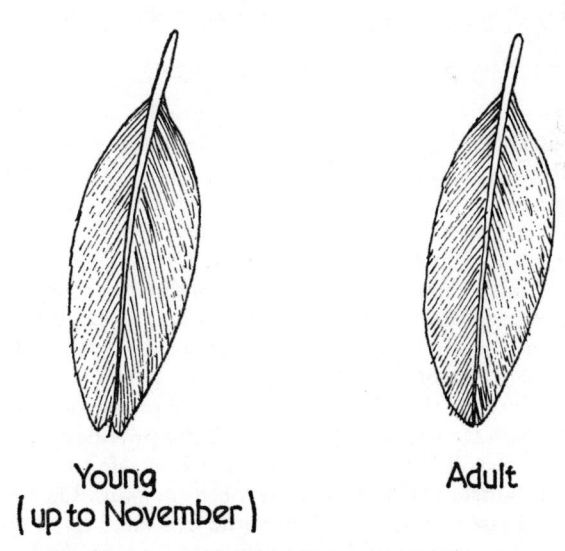

**Young
(up to November)**   **Adult**

Fig 5 Ageing ducks and geese by tail feathers

empties on a bad day and drop them surreptitiously in the next butt. Keepers often go round afterwards to count the empties! Incidentally, if I am shooting grouse and I find a lot of empties in my butt I anticipate a good drive. But if I'm wildfowling and I find a lot of fresh empties, I move on to another place. Ducks are very wary of the place where they were shot at yesterday.

Few people know how to pick out young geese and ducks, when the bag is laid out, unless the plumage is very juvenile. The tail feathers are a reliable guide up to mid-November (see Figure 5).

There are very few rough shoots where one or more flight ponds cannot be constructed, or existing pools or lakes improved. Improvements to existing pools may be by enlargement, or by levelling steep banks and making shallows. Improving lakes is usually a matter of planting cover, making islands or rafts, and of course siting butts (see Figure 6).

Before making a pond a number of important considerations arise. First, the availability of the land. With the high value of land today it is not always easy to find an available site. On the

---

Fig 6   Butting flight ponds
1 Five butts, for three guns, on islands in a square or rectangular pool. Because ducks approach up-wind, three guns with these five positions to choose from can always be placed to face down-wind, whatever the direction of the wind may be.
2 A long pool, with butts for four guns. On a pool 70yd or more in width, butts should not be opposite one another, but staggered. Each gun can then shoot safely at low ducks flying up the centre of the pool when they are directly opposite. They will tend to flare up over one of the guns on the other side. The arrows show safe directions for shooting. If the butts are placed opposite, ducks passing down the centre of the pool will not provide a safe shot for anyone: they will be out of range when it is safe to take them in front, and unsafe when in range between the guns. On a narrower pool, *two* butts may be placed opposite one another, as the ducks will come into range well before they pass between the butts.

Wrong

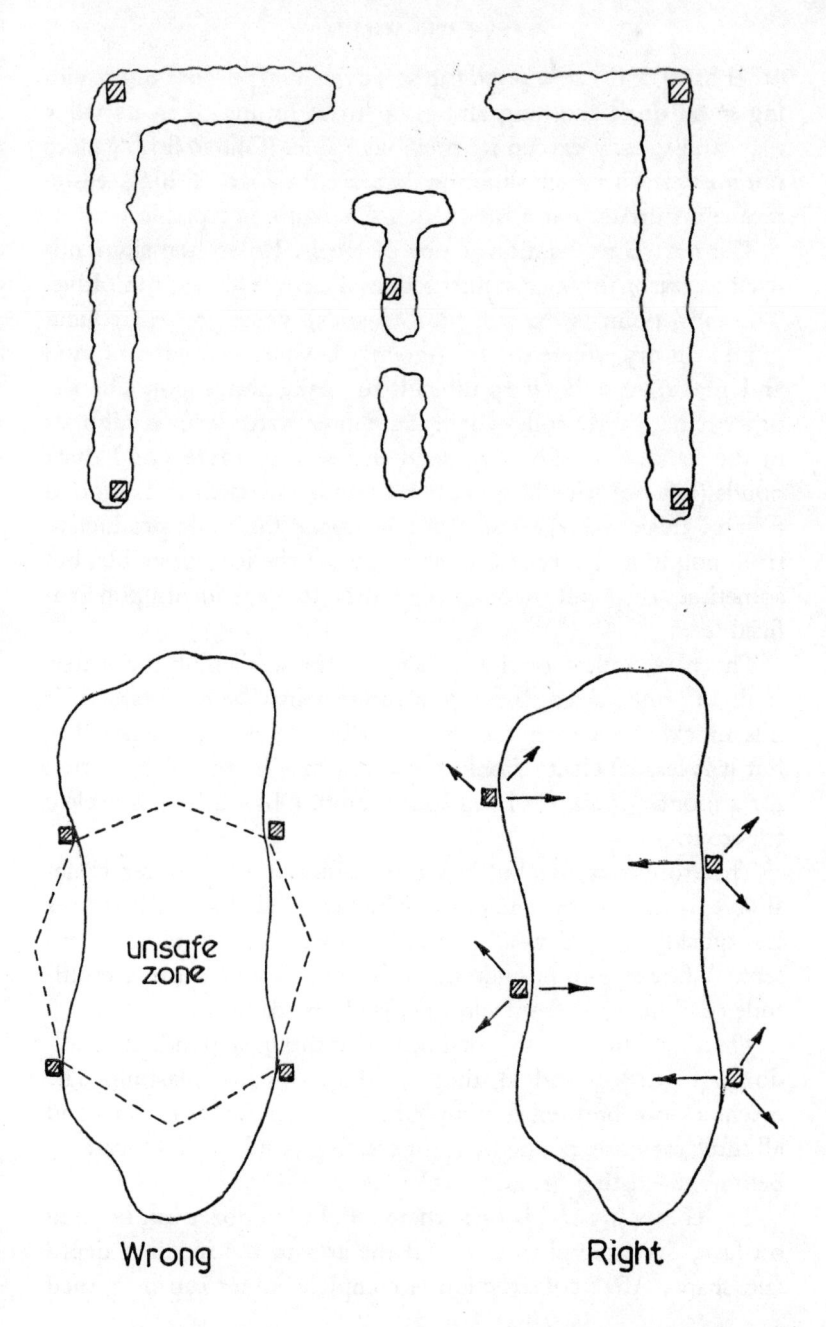

Right

other hand, if the new pond can serve the dual purpose of providing good duck shooting and good trout fishing, then its value may well greatly exceed its previous value. (Coarse fishing does not go well with duck shooting, because the coarse fishing season means disturbance at a time when this is not acceptable.)

The next consideration is one of levels. Unless the site lends itself to reasonably easy construction, the cost will be prohibitive. The third point is the soil. Porous soils, which are so frequent in hill country, where the Ice Age may have left moraines of sand and gravel, can be very difficult to make watertight. On the other hand, sandy soils where the winter water level is high, as in the flats and hollows of sand dunes, may make good duck ponds (but not usually good trout ponds unless there is a good flow of fresh water). Base-rich soils make the most productive trout ponds, and very acid duck ponds are the least desirable, but sometimes they will succeed, when they are dependent upon artificial feed.

The next, rather obvious, factor is the availability of water. A flight pond which dries up in summer may be acceptable if it fills quickly in winter (as many shallow pans and flashes do), but it is less efficient, if only because it may be out of operation for a month or six weeks in the autumn. Obviously it is useless for trout.

Therefore a steady but not too prolific flow of water is desirable, spring water being especially favoured, because it freezes less quickly in hard weather and it is often rich in mineral content. A fast stream is undesirable because it may cause a multitude of difficulties, from silting up to burst dams.

There are three basic methods of creating a pond: by bulldozer (Figures 7 and 8), dragline (Figure 9), or blasting. The machines can be used for impounding water (ie by a dam) and all three methods can be used for creating ponds to hold water—below the existing ground level.

The cheapest pond is one where a light bulldozer can be used on firm, dry ground to doze out the area to the required depth and shape. After construction is complete, water can be turned

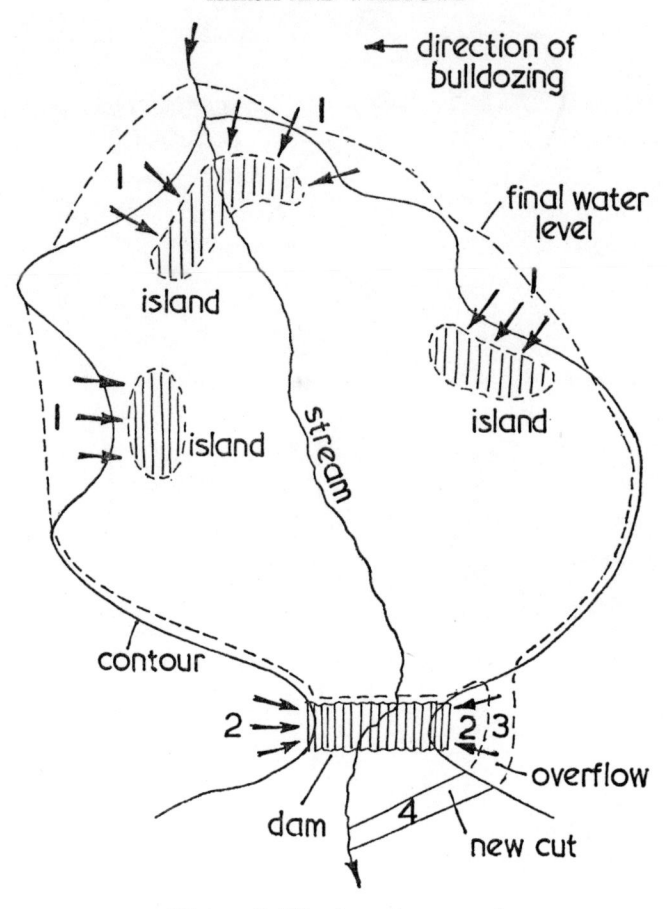

Fig 7   Bulldozing a large pool
1 Bulldoze ground above contour to enlarge area of water and to make islands. *2* Bulldoze dam. *3* Construct wide overflow on solid ground. *4* Cut new line for outflow, well away from dam.

in by a single trench, or leat, controlled as necessary at source. The most expensive one is a deep peat bog, where any machine is almost certain to become bogged for many hours. But such peat areas can be blasted efficiently and cheaply, although pure peat does not make an attractive pool for ducks or fish.

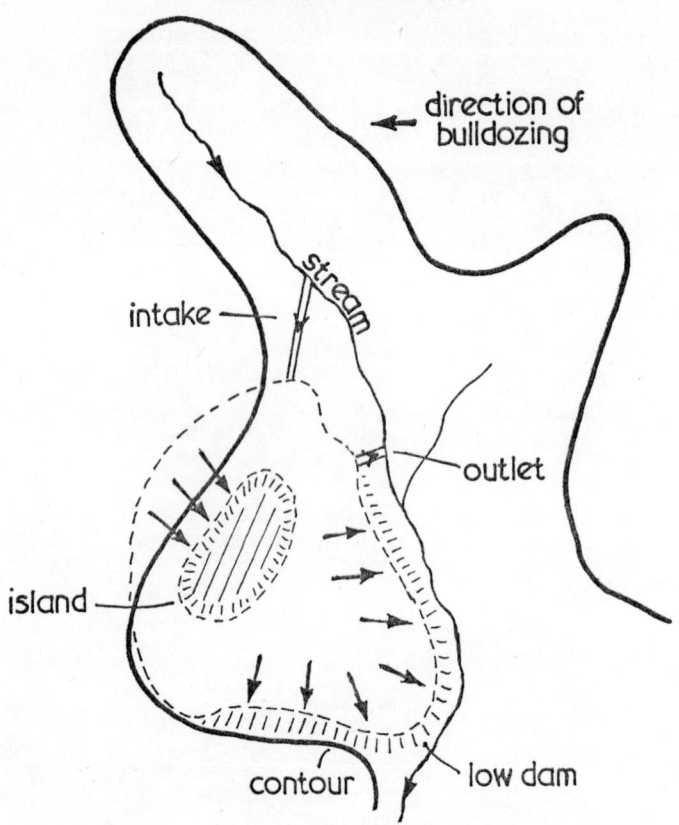

Fig 8 Bulldozing a pool on dry ground

One major problem is the spoil. Diagrams of how to make ponds conveniently skate over this problem, but it can be quite important as high mounds are unsightly and levelling adds quite a lot to the cost, while moving spoil twice is very costly. Some spoil will be needed for islands. Planning the disposal of the spoil is really more important than the precise shape of the pond. Indeed, some latitude is necessary, since unforeseen hazards may be encountered (eg deep pockets of unstable ground or immovable hard rock outcrops) and it is better to alter the shape somewhat than to incur heavy costs in overcoming such obstacles. Square ponds are ugly, although mechanically efficient.

High banks are dangerous for ducklings, which will drown or become chilled if they cannot climb out. Ducks of all ages should be able to swim on to suitable shelves of firm ground. However, a high bank of spoil is acceptable in places, especially where the pond would otherwise be exposed to severe winds; but steep banks erode quickly. The shelter can be improved by planting. Also, the construction of butts is easy in banks of spoil, where they can be made to look entirely natural. Nevertheless, there must be plenty of shallow bays for ducks and some waters of 5–6ft for trout. Diving ducks need deep water, too.

When making a long dam the problem of spoil may be the opposite to that of disposal from excavations: it may become difficult to find enough spoil. Recently, when constructing a single dam to create a three-quarter-acre flight pond, I had to leave before the job was quite finished. The 'dozer driver had only two hours' work to do to complete the dam the next day, but it took him six and a quarter hours because he struck an unforeseen outcrop of solid rock. As a result he had to move spoil from the farthest end, rather than the nearest.

In surveying an area before making a pond it is not necessary to take levels with a theodolite or dumpy. A simple instrument such as the Abney level or even the pocket reflecting level, as supplied by Messrs W. F. Stanley & Co Ltd of New Eltham, London SE9, is perfectly adequate.

A safe rule of thumb is to make the width of the top of the dam approximately equal to the height. The base should be about five times the height. The water level must never rise so that it spills over the bank, and a good safety margin must be left. It follows that the overflow must be wide enough to take the maximum possible flood-water, and it must be constructed on solid, firm ground at the side and not over the dam, otherwise trouble will ensue. If rainbow trout are to be used for stocking, a grid must be put at the overflow to contain them. Wave action may damage the dam; baffles of floating poles, held four feet out from the dam, will obviate this.

The levelling instrument will indicate how far the land behind the dam will be flooded. So often all the work that is done is the completion of the dam. But the area of water can be greatly increased by some dozing at the top end, and possibly bays at the side. This should be done before the dam is made or at least before it is completed, whilst the water has not yet been impounded. The spoil from this work should be moved inwards, so as to form islands.

When a dragline is to be used it is advisable to work off mats if there is any risk at all of bogging. Working off mats adds to the cost, but getting de-bogged may cause crippling costs. Any contractor who is asked to estimate for the work has to cover himself against the risk of bogging. I prefer an hourly rate with close supervision to ensure that bogging is avoided. Even so, accidents can happen, usually owing to lack of communication with the driver, because the noise of the machine drowns conversation. If a lot of work has to be done, a walkie-talkie set would be useful. The RB 24 dragline is a big machine which moves a great deal of soil. I know of a trout lake of 4 acres of an average depth of 4ft excavated by such a machine in five days.

When blasting pools the operator requires a Home Office licence and the police must be notified. The site must be well away from windows. Houses in the vicinity should be notified, otherwise alarm and despondency may be created, and ridiculous claims received. I have known claims relating to aborting donkeys, cracked ceilings and neurotic wives, all of which waste much time!

Gelignite or dynamite are not suitable for constructing pools. They tend to make deep, narrow holes, ideal for trapping wildfowlers in the dark, but not much use for ducks.

The best explosive for making ponds is porous prilled ammonium nitrate, mixed on the spot with 10 per cent diesel oil, in a watertight plastic bag. This charge, which only needs to be placed in a shallow hollow without tamping, is detonated by fuse and detonator in the usual way. It will blow out a shallow oval pan 20ft × 10ft. A series of blasts can be arranged to blow out

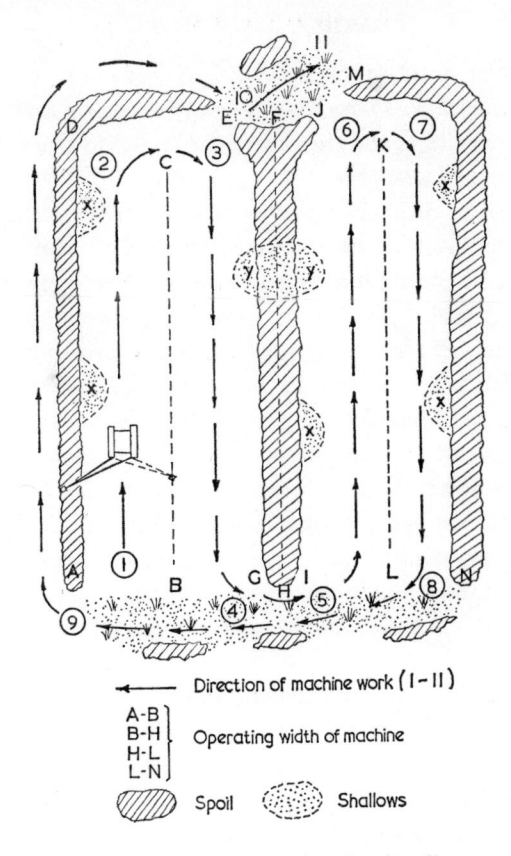

Fig 9   Pool construction by dragline

The machine starts at the point marked 1, excavating from B and putting spoil at A. At points marked X spoil must be sloped down to enable ducklings to climb out of the water. On the first run the machine excavates AB–CD, and on the return CF–BH.

From 5 to 6, spoil is placed at HI–FJ. At points marked Y spoil is left shallow for ducklings. Machine ends main excavation at 8.

From 8 to 9 machine takes out shallow scoops 9in deep, leaving clumps of natural vegetation. Finally, machine moves from 9 to 10 without working and then makes similar shallows from 10 to 11.

The banks and islands can be planted with low shrubs—dogwoods, cotoneasters, spireas, etc—to provide nesting cover and to hide butts.

The length of the pool may be extended as far as the lie of the land permits, and its width may be extended by repeating the process outside M–N.

a sizeable area, and, if they are arranged in a circle, an island will be left in the middle. There is a tendency for the spoil to be thrown into a shallow ridge, and this may need some tidying up by hand, or by machine if available.

The question of planting up ponds requires consideration. A newly made pool is an unattractive eyesore. But too much shrubbery and trees will be a nuisance in later years. Protection is needed on the exposed sides to provide shelter from the prevailing wind. But open flyways for duck are most desirable. Ducks which have to come in down a sort of wide chimney in a canopy of trees will find as great a difficulty in doing so as the guns will have in shooting them. Teal are very agile on the wing, but I have known them find it impossible to drop in to a small pond in a strong gale, when a tall oak tree interfered with their up-wind approach. So it is necessary to visualise what any planting will look like in 20-30 years' time.

The following trees and shrubs are useful under the right conditions.

For wide open lakes, or marshes, where it is desirable to funnel the flight lines to butts—poplars, *Poplar tricocarpa* × *tachomahaka* being one of the best, or *Alnus cordata*, a very fast-growing alder. These will grow quickly and, if gaps of 60yd are left, ducks will pass through the gap and over a butt placed in the centre.

For amenity, clumps of golden willow, white poplars, cherries and snowy mespilus are good, and weeping willows are suitable for large islands. Hornbeam produces seed which is eaten.

Berried species of some value include the mountain ash, although the berries, ripe in late August, are too early for benefit. Stransvesia and *Cotoneaster frigidus* bear profuse berries, which are ripe at Christmas, when food is short.

Low ground cover can be provided by a variety of shrubs. *Cornus sibirica*, westonbirt form, has vivid scarlet branches in winter. *Spiraea salicifolia* will stand wet, acid conditions. Sea buckthorn (*Hippophae rhamnoides*) has pleasant grey foliage. It is dioecious, the yellow berries being carried on the female plants only. On sandy soils it will spread fast. In the north juniper is a useful bush, as is broom. Tree lupin is another useful shrub for light soils. *Cotoneaster microphylla* or *C. horizontalis* make suitable nesting cover for ducks.

In a new flight pond it is a mistake to introduce bulrush or the Norfolk reed (*Phragmites*). They will colonise too much open water. But there are four water plants which should be introduced before other types of vegetation have colonised the banks. Burreed (*Sparganium*) will grow in the margins if not too peaty. The seed, carried on green burr-like heads, is much sought after by teal and mallard. Amphibious bistort (*Polygonum bistorta*) and broadleaved pondweed grow submerged, with floating leaves and flowers. Both are excellent. Water crowfoot (*Ranunculus peltatus*) is useful because it harbours shrimps and snails. For trout *Elodia crispa* is excellent, but it requires an alkaline silt.

The best way to raise the alkalinity of a pool is to pack the intake with limestone. This will create a zone where shrimps and other trout food will breed and disperse into the pool. It is not practical to make a very large lake alkaline.

A lake of more than 5 million gallons requires a special licence, and the local river authority should be consulted for this or for cases where the flow of water is impeded or reduced. As already stated, a Home Office licence is required for blasting.

Marshland which is grazed by cattle or horses is especially attractive to snipe because of the worms in the droppings. Snipe habitat can be improved by making a number of quite small puddles, say 2yd × 1yd, pepper-potted throughout the area. Snipe are liable to vary in number throughout the season. They do not like stale marshland. During hard frost they will be concentrated at running springs. Many are forced to leave the area.

Because snipe are small birds, it is often thought that they take less notice of danger than, say, pheasants. This is a fallacy. For every snipe which rises within shot, ten will take off out of range, especially if the guns and dogs are noisy. It is often more productive to drive them than to walk up. If the area is studied, it is usually easy to place the guns on the natural flight line. As with ducks, it is most important for the forward guns to take up positions quietly and unobtrusively and to be reasonably concealed. Wild dogs and loud-voiced sportsmen are just as great a menace on a snipe bog as anywhere else on a shoot. When snipe have been driven off a particularly favourite habitat, some will return quite soon, sometimes even before the drive is over.

The old question of whether to walk up snipe down-wind or up-wind is a vexed one. So much depends upon the natural line of approach. When walking down-wind, snipe which get up within shot present easier shots, but more will go away out of shot. An up-wind snipe is more difficult. My own preference is to work across the wind, back and forth, starting at the down-wind end of the marsh. During periods of full moon snipe may be found well away from their normal haunts, in such unlikely places as turnip fields.

Few rough shoots will include saltmarshes or tidal areas. But tide and wind make considerable impact upon duck shoots in coastal areas. For instance, a gale will make ducks leave the open tideway as the tide comes in, especially at the times of the spring tides. Then they will seek the shelter of inland lakes and pools, and under such conditions morning flight may be prolonged throughout the morning. But after spring tides there may be many attractive flashes left on the saltings at low tide, and these will hive off some of the ducks which would come to the flight pond under other conditions.

Of course, on tidal areas, a daytime tide flight may be had as the ducks are brought in by wave and wind. There are strategic places for tide flights on every shoreline.

Tide tables may be obtained from Messrs Mackenzie and Storrie of Leith, and every fowler of tidal areas should possess a copy. Spring tides, which come in higher and go out farther, occur at the periods of the new and full moon. Neap tides, which have the least rise and fall, occur at the periods between full and new moon. It is essential for every shooter on tidal areas to understand the general movements of tide and current and, especially, the particular behaviour of wind, tide and wave in his precise locality. His sport will depend upon this knowledge, and there are times when his life may depend upon it.

6
Deer on the Rough Shoot

In England (and in parts of Wales) deer are increasing, both in numbers and range, largely owing to the increased habitats provided by the wide-scale planting of woodland and forests, both private and state. In particular, fallow deer and roe are extending their range quite fast, whilst sika, and to a lesser extent red deer, are spreading slowly from their few main centres. Muntjac have also spread from Woburn as far as Gloucestershire and Dorset, perhaps farther.

In Scotland, roe have always been numerous and they colonise new plantations very quickly. Red deer are very numerous in the Highlands and the Galloway hills. Sika are also present in a number of localities and they are extending their range quite rapidly. Only fallow seem to be relatively static around the few areas where they have been established.

In view of these facts, it is obvious that deer may turn up on many rough shoots. Sometimes the presence of occasional deer is quite unsuspected, because deer often become established before there is any local knowledge of deer behaviour or habits. When they are discovered, all too often ignorance leads to inhumane methods of slaughter.

Although it is legal to shoot deer with 12-bore shotguns, loaded with SSG or larger shot, there are many good reasons why this practice should be discontinued. In the excitement of the moment there is a great temptation to fire at too great a distance: often only the backside is seen and a shot will wound, or maim, without killing; at other angles it is all too easy for a pellet to blind one eye, or injure one ear. Deer are strong animals and they will carry a lot of shot and either die slowly, or recover painfully, over a long period. A very strong reason against the use of a gun is that it is but rarely possible to be selective. Young deer which should be left to mature may be shot: the ringleader of marauding deer (which is the one to eliminate) may escape, and, in the case of roe bucks, the master buck may be shot, leaving territories to be split up amongst lesser bucks, each of which will do vastly greater damage to trees than the master buck was doing. A master buck holds a large territory and has little need to throw his weight about. Teenage bucks *have* to make a great effort to assert themselves and in doing so cause great damage to young trees.

Therefore, whatever may be the temptation to have a deer drive, it is preferable—very greatly preferable—that deer should be treated with respect, as the prime beast of the chase, and shot only by rifles of a suitable calibre (·240 and larger, except in Scotland where the treble 2 is legal). The ·243 is a wonderful all-round rifle, though for red deer, only, perhaps a larger calibre is desirable. Above all, the temptation to loose off at a deer with small shot (illegally) at a pheasant drive must be abhorred.

Lucky indeed is the owner of a rough shoot which carries a stock of deer. Properly managed they will provide him with many hours of pleasure and excellent sport with a rifle, much of it outside the game season. The legal open seasons for shooting deer are shown in the table below.

Deer Open Seasons (dates inclusive)

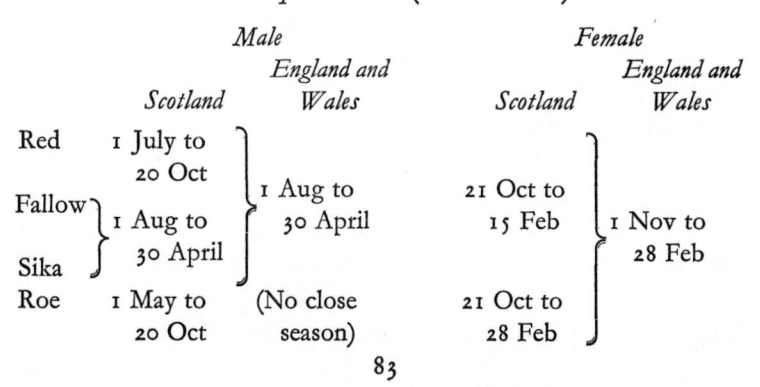

	Male		Female	
	Scotland	England and Wales	Scotland	England and Wales
Red	1 July to 20 Oct	1 Aug to 30 April	21 Oct to 15 Feb	1 Nov to 28 Feb
Fallow	1 Aug to 30 April	1 Aug to 30 April	21 Oct to 15 Feb	1 Nov to 28 Feb
Sika	1 Aug to 30 April	1 Aug to 30 April	21 Oct to 15 Feb	1 Nov to 28 Feb
Roe	1 May to 20 Oct	(No close season)	21 Oct to 28 Feb	

How does one go about shooting deer with a rifle? The experienced deer man will know what to do, so the following notes are for the benefit of those who find themselves with a stock of deer on their shoot and no very clear idea about the best means to take advantage of them—with a rifle.

First of all, it is essential to have an intimate knowledge of the ground. This is more important in the case of deer than with any other quarry. How often when stalking a roe buck have I thought that I knew the area very well! How often have I been wrong, because I have overlooked a fold in the ground, and not made allowance for a curl in the wind caused by local topography —or just because the deer knew every inch better than I (as he is almost certain to do).

Secondly, one must study the deer and get to know their habits intimately.

Thirdly, one must learn to move very slowly and silently, remembering always that a deer is much more alert than a human being; that an alerted deer is possessed of greater patience than the average human being—by which I mean that if both deer and man suspect the other's presence, it is usually the man who will move first and thus give himself away; that in woodland conditions a deer's eyes are at the level of a man's knees—therefore a deer can see a man's legs moving under the general level of the branches, when the deer is hidden from the man's eyes by the foliage; above all else, that a deer's hearing is acute, and its scenting ability second to none, and that, when it is using either faculty, it can pinpoint the source of sound, or scent, to a square yard—it will know exactly where you are.

When studying the behaviour of deer the most useful asset is a keen power of observation. Here, the dew has been dispersed, or the grass flattened by the passage of a deer. There, the slots on bare ground will give information as to species, age, sex and size, and the manner of its passing. For instance, all male deer move with their feet pointing slightly outwards: therefore their slots will be the same. All female deer leave their slots in a straight line. A running deer will leave an imprint with his cleaves wide apart.

DEER ON THE ROUGH SHOOT

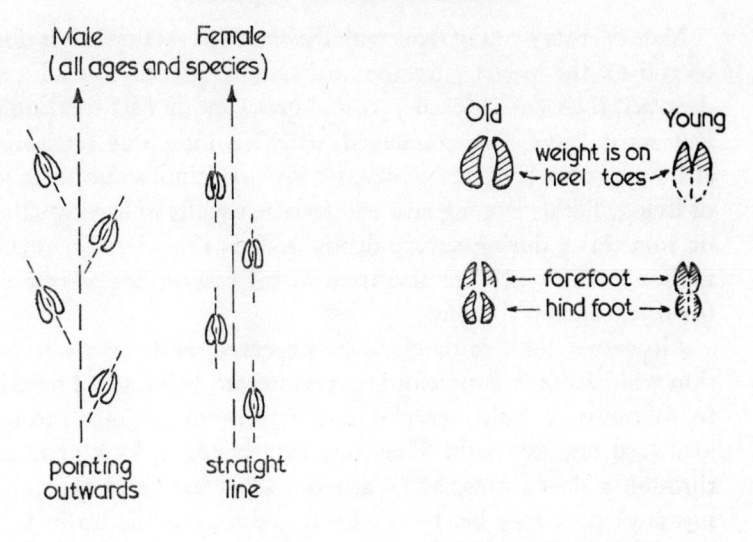

Male (all ages and species) — pointing outwards
Female — straight line

Old — weight is on heel
Young — weight is on toes
forefoot
hind foot

Walking/trotting
— forefoot
— hind foot

Cantering or galloping
— cleaves wide apart
— dew claws (not always visible)

Fig 10 Basic information from deer slots

Twigs, buds, leaves, grass, etc must all be inspected, for the only sign that deer have been present may be the browsed shoots. If there are many deer there will be a 'browse line' below which they have reached up to eat most of the leaves and twigs. If there are but a few deer, there will be the odd tip of a bramble or wild rose shoot missing—for all deer eat both with relish. In winter ivy growing up a tree will be leafless as high as a deer can reach. It is necessary to distinguish between twigs eaten by deer and those eaten by rabbits and hares. Deer, having no upper front teeth, leave a slightly fractured or torn skin. Hares and rabbits cut cleanly as with a pair of secateurs.

Male deer fray young trees with their antlers. At first this is done to rub off the velvet after the antlers have grown (for all male deer cast their antlers each year and grow another set thereafter). But most fraying is connected with marking out territories, although some is done in play, or just to demonstrate their joy of living. Bark stripping also takes place, usually in hard weather, or sometimes during severe drought. It is done by the outside incisor teeth, which are also used to eat cast antlers and bones, for their calcium content.

Altogether there is much to be observed, and one's observation will become a source of intense interest. It is a good practice to follow deer paths, even if this may mean pushing through awkward undergrowth. Thus one may begin to look at things through a deer's eyes, and learn quickly what the local movements of deer may be. Generally speaking, deer lie up in thick cover during the day and come out to feed in the evening. They will be abroad very early in the morning and that is the best time of all to observe them. When they are lying up it is not easy to see them before they see you. But it is easy to intercept them between their resting-places and their feeding-ground, provided the wind is favourable.

Often they feed in fields, where they are obvious and easily seen. But in woodlands they will be found in open glades and felled areas (or newly replanted areas) and on rides at feeding times.

In order to see deer it is usually more productive to take up a position on a point of vantage and to remain still and silent, rather than to cover a large area looking for them on foot. But if it is decided to stalk, then the early morning is preferable because the deer will already be out and about. If one stalks in the evening, one may pass through before the deer are on their feet.

When stalking it is absolutely essential to move very slowly. It is a sad and unfortunate fact that many human beings have lost the art of moving silently. A beginner may think that he has to walk on tiptoe. Nothing is farther from the truth. When stalking, the heel of the foot must touch the ground first. Thereafter the sole of the foot is lowered slowly, the whole weight being on the one foot already positioned, and the heel of the other. If a twig, or stone, or uncomfortable unevenness is felt as the sole is lowered, then a new position for the heel must be found before the whole foot becomes firmly placed. A walking-stick helps to maintain balance, the ideal being a thumb-stick with a wide cleft. This is of great value when taking a standing shot, for the elbow, or forearm, according to the height required, is placed in the fork and that gives a large measure of steadiness. Of course the rifle must never be rested on the thumb-stick, or directly on any hard object, as that leads to a certain miss, through flip.

All deer are basically woodland animals, even though the 'deer forest' of red deer is a stretch of open hill ground mostly devoid of trees. That is because it is the only habitat which man has left vacant for deer. They prefer true forest conditions and grow heavier and carry heavier antlers under forest conditions, because of better shelter and feed. On the other hand, the roe deer, although a true woodland species, may be found on open moorland. I have seen a roe at 2,000ft, two miles from any tree. That is partly because they have been pushed out of the woodlands by stronger members of their own race. This happens to the young roe. Fallow are not often found far from woodland or scrub, but sika use the open hill ground frequently.

Great ignorance about identifying deer is often shown. The main differences are most easily seen in their backsides, which is fortunate, because that is what is most frequently seen!

Roe, the smallest deer, except for muntjac, are not much larger than a big dog. They stand 26in at the withers. From the rear, they show a large white caudal patch (ie on the rump). The tail is rudimentary and invisible, but the female carries a short anal tuft, white or buff, which is a distinctive feature. In summer the coat is a rich foxy red: in winter, mouse-colour. Roe bucks carry only six-point antlers, which average 8in. Anything over $9\frac{1}{2}$in is exceptional.

Fallow have a half-moon-shaped caudal patch and the longest tail of all—9in, black on top, white below. In summer it is moving continuously to keep away flies, and that movement gives them away. The coat is variable, the normal being mouse-colour in winter and a spotted brown in summer, but black, menil (very pale with many spots) and white are all normal variations. The bucks carry antlers which are palmated.

Red stags have wide-spreading antlers with brow, bez and trey tines and, when perfect, a cup on top, thus giving a royal or twelve-point head. Royals are not numerous although exceptionally more than twelve points are carried. Red deer are the largest of all British deer. The coat colour varies much, being sometimes buffish brown, and more often dun. The tail is 5in, reddish brown, with a buff caudal patch.

Often sika deer are thought to be very small. This is not so. The stags are solid, heavy deer weighing very little less than fallow bucks. In winter they look black, but the coat is really a silver black, rather like a silver fox. The hind is mouse-colour in winter. Both sexes have a distinctive grey 'V' on the face. The tail is slightly longer than a red deer's, about 6in, but markedly shorter than a fallow's tail. The rump is white and can be confused only with roe. (The only other deer which looks black in winter is the black fallow, but they have black rumps and black tails which should prevent any confusion in identification.) In summer the sika coat is a dull chestnut-red with a dappling of faint spots. Hinds have slightly shorter ears than fallow or red.

Having studied the movements and behaviour of the deer on a rough shoot, plans must be made for shooting. One must decide where it is safe to use a rifle from the ground (that is, where there is a safe background beyond the deer: a mound, or higher bank sufficient to take any possible ricochet of the bullet). Where it is not safe, a high seat must be put up, so that one will be firing downwards at an angle steep enough for the ground to absorb the bullet. There are other advantages of a high seat, other than the very important one of safety. It is much easier to see deer from a high seat and to get a clear shot. Sometimes, too, when the wind is adverse, one's scent may be carried above the level of the deer. Deer are used to predators which come upon them at ground level, and even though most of these predators are no longer present in Britain, deer are accustomed to seeing men, dogs and foxes (which will take newly born roe kids or fawns) on the ground. Therefore, they tend not to look upwards. But of course that does not mean that one can move about freely on a high seat. One must sit still. Indeed, the best advice ever given is carved on an ancient seat in the New Forest. 'Sit still, look long and hold yourself quiet', a simple formula, but not so easy for the beginner to follow.

The secret of sitting still is to dispose oneself in a comfortable position, and then relax. If one is sitting on the ground at a point of vantage which will be used regularly, it is desirable to dig a hole for one's feet. If one is on a high seat, it is essential that one's feet should be supported. (They must not be hanging in mid-air as that becomes most uncomfortable very quickly.) It is desirable to have a back-rest. It is useful to be sitting upon a game bag, or folded mackintosh. With feet and back supported, one can remain motionless for a long time. If one thinks one hears something or if one catches a movement out of the corner of one's eye, there is an almost irresistible temptation to turn one's head quickly in order to get a view. But one's head must be turned *slowly*: one's field glasses must be raised to the eyes *slowly*: if one smokes, one's hand must move the cigarette to and from the lips *slowly*: even flies must be swatted *slowly*! And at last, when the moment comes to shoot, after the deer has been carefully studied so that one knows as much as possible about the quarry (ie whether it is male or female, old or young, shootable or not) the rifle must be raised *slowly*. Shooting from a sitting position is easiest of all, for one's elbows can rest firmly on one's knees. When shooting from the right shoulder one can cover a wider field of fire to the left than to the right. Therefore, one should sit facing about two o'clock, assuming the deer is expected to come from twelve o'clock. But of course probably it will come from a different direction. If it is far to the right, then one cannot bring the rifle to bear without moving one's position somewhat.

I am often asked: 'I suppose I must not smoke?' If a deer can smell cigarette smoke it will be able to smell the hated human scent even more readily, so smoking can only be a disadvantage in that it causes some movement of the hand. In dry weather the risk of starting a forest fire must be remembered and then it is better not to smoke. On the open hill an old red hind may see the smoke and be alerted, but in woodland conditions, where deer are used to the natural movement of leaves and branches, when blown by wind, they do not take much notice of smoke. So, I smoke when I feel like it, or when I am eaten by midges, or when I want to see exactly how the wind is eddying—the last being the best excuse! It is very desirable to have some insect repellent, too.

A deer seat may be a simple board placed across a suitable fork in a tree, with a ladder: or it may have to be a free-standing four-post structure. Some pruning of branches, or clearing of scrub, is nearly always necessary. It is a good idea for one person to move round in a circle, about 100yd from the seat, from which another person decides what it is necessary to remove in order to get a clear view. One twig, or one leaf, or even long grass will cause a modern high-powered soft-nosed bullet to expand too soon or become totally deflected.

At last comes the moment for the shot. Do not aim at the head. A bullet may be only a trifle off-target, and then the beast may be hit in the lower jaw. An animal so wounded is likely to escape, travelling a long distance, and dying very slowly of starvation. The neck shot brings instant death, but a long shot at the neck needs a very expert and accurate marksman. Therefore, the standard shot should be the heart shot. Wait until the beast is broadside on. Once a decision has been made to shoot, the whole process of raising the rifle, picking up the deer in the scope, aiming and squeezing the trigger should not take more than five seconds. Sight the rifle on the back part of the foreleg, then come up the body to a point between one-third and one-half of the body width. Hold steady and squeeze the trigger gently. The shot should find the heart. Usually the deer will rush forward, head outstretched, for a distance of up to 100yd (40yd being about average). It will be found dead, and its last dying rush is painless. If the bullet cuts the arteries at the top of the heart, it will drop dead at once. But any deer which drops to the shot should be assumed wounded until one is certain that it is dead. A bullet grazing the top of the spine, or hitting an antler, will stun the animal. It will recover quite quickly and often get clean away, if one is not prepared for this possibility.

A deer that has been shot should be bled as soon as possible and galloched.

It is a good idea for two, or possibly three, rifles to go out to use high seats at the same time, provided they each know exactly where the others are. There are two good reasons for this. Those observers in the same area should be able to form a much better picture of all deer movements for the evening than one, alone, could do. Also if a heavy beast is shot, the whole party can help to bring it out.

Sometimes it is desirable to 'move' deer to rifles posted in strategic, safe positions. Only one beater who knows the ground intimately is needed. He must move slowly, tapping a tree here and there. If the deer do not stop when within range, a short, sharp whistle will make them halt. It will take between two and five yards for them to stop, so the whistle should be given just before they are in the best position for the shot. This is an efficient method of culling deer in winter.

One should not forget that where deer are numerous, some of them will have been feeding on someone's fields. When a tenant has complained about damage done by deer, a present of a haunch will not come amiss.

7
The Rough Shooter's Dog

An essential item connected with any rough shoot is a dog. To my way of thinking, no shooting day can be complete unless one is able to share it with one's dog, and one of the sad things about some big shoots is that all the picking-up is done by professional pickers-up. If one is emboldened to take one's own dog, he is more of an ornament (or sometimes, if we are honest, a source of worry) than an essential member of the party.

But that is not the case on a rough shoot, for there a dog is an absolute necessity. I would go so far as to say that unless one has a useful dog, it is just not worth while considering renting a rough shoot. One of the great pleasures of rough shooting is the companionship and the mutual enjoyment which comes from the teamwork between man and dog, when both understand each other and work together. No other form of shooting brings out such a high degree of skill and intelligence in dog work, although the standard required may not be quite that of the field trial champion. One's dog must be under reasonable control, but there will be occasions when he may be allowed to do things which might cause consternation at a field trial!

'What sort of a dog?' is the big question. Almost every sort of dog may have a place on a rough shoot. I have seen wonderful work done by dachshunds and even by fox terriers, both of which will hunt the thickest cover better than a spaniel. Every shooting man has his own preference for the sort of shooting dog that he likes above all others. Much depends upon the type of shooting that is done most frequently.

For walking up grouse or other game birds and snipe, on open moorland or marsh, where they are not very plentiful on the ground, a good pointer or setter is ideal. There is an enormous amount of pleasure and a very particular type of excitement when shooting over a good pair of these dogs. Also, of course, a great deal of unproductive walking will be saved by a pointer or setter covering the ground.

The chief difficulty is that the average rough shoot hardly provides enough ground to warrant the keeping of pointers or setters; and unless these dogs are well trained and have plenty of work they can be a menace. The dog that ranges far too widely and then comes to a point where no one can find him is a great nuisance. Worse still is the dog that does not hold to his point. It is exasperating to have the quarry flushed just before the guns are within range!

On the whole I do not think that either pointers or setters provide the ideal answer for the rough shoot, except where the shoot has a very large acreage of indifferent grouse moor.

If the rough shoot has a fairly large proportion of thick cover —scrub woodland, broom or gorsey banks, brambles, etc— there is little doubt that a good working spaniel is ideal for finding and flushing game, combined with retrieving after the shot. English and Welsh springers seem to me to have rather more drive than the other spaniel breeds.

If the shoot is predominantly a wildfowl area, especially if there are deep, wide creeks and rivers to be crossed and much open water, then I think that a labrador is the ideal dog. There is little to choose between the black or yellow, or the retrievers, the golden or flatcoat, or curly coat. The last is a splendid water dog. So too is the Irish water spaniel, so much more like a retriever than a spaniel. Which of the various retriever breeds to choose is probably a matter of personal preference, provided the pup comes from a good, reputable working strain that is free from congenital blindness and hip displacia.

Finally there are certain continental breeds which are all-purpose dogs. The German pointer, the weinerama and the Hungarian vizsla are all splendid dogs. Perhaps they may be a little headstrong and require extra careful handling, but I know no other breeds which can be said to be the jack of all shooting trades. They will work cover like a spaniel, point as well as an English pointer, retrieve, follow a wounded deer very efficiently, and hunt a winged duck or goose in water as well as a labrador. They may suffer from cold in really severe hard weather, when wet, but they are outstandingly bold and brave. I have never owned one, but I have worked closely with a German pointer bitch and few dogs have impressed me more. In woodland a small bell should be attached to the collar, so that contact can be maintained.

My own personal choice is a labrador. But that is because I put wildfowling first, and a good labrador or retriever makes the best water dog. A labrador will work rough cover very well, but I would not claim that these dogs are as good as spaniels or German pointers for working cover and putting up or 'setting' game.

No one should despise a half-bred dog. Often a first cross has many of the best points from both parents. The first dog I ever had was said to be a cross between a clumber and an English springer. He looked like a cross between a pointer and a terrier. He taught me more about dogs, and about working a rough shoot to the best advantage, than any subsequent experience has done.

It is said that if one is lucky one may have one first-class dog in a lifetime. Mine was given to me by a forester, many years ago, the dog's mother being the forester's black labrador bitch of exceptional intelligence. His father was said to be one of the blue-blooded labradors from 'the Hall'. He was the runt of the litter, a tiny black pup with beady black eyes. (Often it is best to pick the smallest of a litter of pups, because he will have had to use his brain from the very start, to outwit his larger brothers and sisters when suckling the bitch!) He never looked quite pure, and when I met the forester many years later and showed him the 'Wog', as he was called, the forester, having forgotten about the alleged father from the Hall, stood back and said: 'Well, fancy him turning out like that—his father was only the parson's old terrier.' I told that story to a well-known judge who was a great dog man. He said at once, 'All I can say is that the parson ought to have been made a bishop!' He had the greatest respect and regard for the dog, and once, when the old dog in his last year had done a particularly good retrieve, the judge turned to his own six spaniels and addressed them as follows: 'There, the old man is worth the whole of you lot put together. He's the best dog in the world.'

Certainly he was the best dog I have ever known and he knew more about shooting than many a man who goes out with a gun. He always knew a wounded bird, even, quite frequently, when I thought I had missed. If it came down it was in the bag—I never had to worry about it. He would suit his behaviour to the type of shooting day. If we were shooting pheasants, he would lie beside my shooting-stick, as good as gold. If I was flighting ducks, he would slip away and retrieve each one as it fell, with no fuss or commotion. If we were shooting rabbits he would hunt them as a terrier would. If I was flighting on the open shore I would put him out as a flanker, maybe a hundred yards from me.

It is very difficult to keep under perfect control any dog which is used for working cover and putting up game. If such a dog is under complete control, he may lack drive, whereas the dog with the greatest energy and the most fearless drive for facing thick cover may have to be forgiven if he goes to collect a winged cock pheasant the moment the bird hits the ground. Indeed on a rough shoot, with only a few birds to be outwitted, the sooner a runner is collected the better. On the other hand, the dog that tears off into the blue every time a shot is fired is just as large a menace on the rough shoot as he is at the big shoot.

It is infuriating to see the only three cock pheasants on the area pushed over the boundary fence, when one is shooting by oneself. But it is even more embarrassing to see one's dog flushing pheasants in the middle of the next drive in front of a whole team of guns. So immediate obedience to the whistle is essential.

It is a great mistake for a working dog to be required to answer to his name in the shooting field. An irate gun bellowing his dog's name with full lung-power is likely to move far more birds in the shortest possible time, over the widest possible area, than the wildest dog. Let commands be by hand signal or by a gentle hiss if the dog is close, an oral whistle if he is farther out, and an Acme whistle if he is in the remote distance. An Acme whistle is silent, so, with luck, no one will know that your dog is not taking the slightest notice of it!

Your dog should be trained to walk to heel. He must sit when told and lie, or drop, when required, and remain for as long as need be. This is essential when one is in a duck hide or pigeon hide. It is essential that he should walk on a lead without pulling, especially when game flushes at his feet. If a dog that is a little bit unreliable when working off the lead will behave quietly on the lead, then he may be taken to any shoot. He must retrieve with a gentle mouth and follow a runner as long as scent holds good.

Some dogs do not like retrieving woodcock or snipe. But if they are started off on a dead jackdaw, jay or magpie, when they are being trained, they will carry anything in later life.

As Jorrocks said: 'There's nothing so queer as scent, 'cept a woman.' A dog knows more about scent than any human being can possibly know. How often people display their total ignorance of matters affecting scent. How often a dog is recalled time and time again to the place where his master *thinks* the bird may be, when the dog has already started to follow the scent elsewhere. How often one sees guns and beaters trampling all over the ground where a bird has fallen, thus foiling the scent very effectively! One should stand down-wind, or to the side, and give the dog every chance to make the best use of his nose.

I was brought up never to give a dog cheese at lunchtime in case the strong smell interfered with the dog's scenting powers. I am inclined to think that this is not so very important. Just as human beings who work under conditions of strong smells quickly become oblivious to the smell, so dogs also experience 'nasal fatigue' as this is called. It may happen in as little as two minutes, if the scent is very strong, but after a thirty-second rest the fatigue will disappear. A faint scent will not cause fatigue, and the fact that one particular strong smell has caused fatigue does not prevent the dog from smelling other scents, so the cheese probably does not matter.

There are certain basic facts which concern scent. H. M. Budgett did an enormous amount of patient research into the subject and in the end he was able to uncover most of the mysteries about scent in his book *Hunting by Scent*, published in 1933 by Eyre & Spottiswoode. Here are some of his main findings which are important to all who use dogs, or hounds, in the sporting field—and for all who stalk wild animals.

Most animals either have scent glands in their feet or sweat through their feet. It is doubtful if game birds have such glands, and it is probable that scent glands in the body impregnate their feathers and that when they squat the scent is transferred to their feet. Any bird or animal, including man, leaves a trail of particles on the ground, and on herbage which the feet have trodden upon, or which the body has touched in passing. Scent is the air which has come into contact with these particles, not the particles themselves. Therefore, obviously, the best scenting conditions are when air currents are carrying the scent towards the dog, and that happens when the air is rising and moving down-wind. This is affected by the climatic conditions of the day, although there appears to be no direct connection between scent and barometric pressure. Hot air rises, therefore scenting conditions are good when the temperature at the ground (that is, immediately below the surface, not at the surface) is higher than that of the air above it.

When the temperature at the ground is lower than that of the air above it there will be little or no scent. In fact the earth absorbs air under these conditions and may be said to breathe. If the temperature of the air and the earth are equal, then scenting conditions will be average.

What are the factors which influence these conditions? Mist or fog occurs when moist ground conditions are at a higher temperature than the air. Also, water vapour retards radiation and there is less loss of heat from the earth. Therefore scenting conditions are good in fog. A night frost after a mild spell means that the air is cool and the ground radiates warmth, and this gives good scenting conditions. At evening there is a general fall in air temperature, thus producing good scenting conditions. This is one reason why many wild animals feed in the early evening and at night: a deer can scent its enemies better than in the heat of the day, but the carnivorous predator can also wind its quarry more easily then. Good scenting conditions aid both, according to their relative positions.

A change from a warm westerly to a cold easterly produces good scenting conditions, likewise if snow falls before a frost the ground remains warm and scent is good. But when snow comes after a frost scent will be bad for some time after the thaw. When there has been a prolonged frost the thaw will be accompanied by mild weather and a warm wind which may reach gale force. This is bad for scent (but good for wildfowling and pigeon shooting). When there is a white hoar frost on the cobwebs the ground temperature will be lower than the air temperature with poor scenting conditions.

One may encounter different scenting conditions at the same time. Thus, in the open, the ground may be warmed by the sun whilst the air is still cooler, and scent will be good. But in covert the shade will keep the ground cool and scent will be poor. The reverse may occur, with the air heated by a warm breeze in the open giving little scent, whilst the air is kept cool by the shade in covert, the soil retaining its heat from the previous day, and this will give good scent. To be more precise, when the air temperature is 2° or 3° warmer than the earth, there will still be a moderate scent. If the air is 5° or 6° warmer, scent will be very poor, and at 10° it will be non-existent.

Conditions change during the day. The earth is not subject to rapid change, 3° or 4° during the day only. But air temperature may change as much as 20°. Heavy rain will obliterate scent and intense cold may retard it. Bright sunlight will obliterate it in several hours. Bright daylight has a deodorising effect, so the best photographic conditions give the worst scenting conditions. It seems obvious from these facts that dogs which compete at field trials either early or late in the day may have a distinct advantage over those being worked around midday.

Certain things add to the difficulties of bad scenting. Thus scent is poor on a newly carted hay field, or where cattle fed on cow cake are present. Rushes and green bracken often hold but little scent. Willowherb in flower, garlic, cuckoo pint, wild mint and mustard crops hold very little scent. Burnt stubbles, and areas close to main roads with much car exhaust, carry but little scent.

The question of how long scent lasts is important and interesting. On average a fox's scent lasts half an hour, a hare's forty-five minutes, a bird's two hours, a man's five hours, a deer's six hours, a boar's twelve hours and an otter's two days—because the scent particles from an otter are very fatty. Of course, blood scent from a wounded animal lasts longer. These times are subject to much variation due to local conditions.

There is another important point concerning scent. Even a light animal passing over grass causes a slight crushing which in turn produces scent particles from the grass. A dog can follow the trail, using the scent from the crushed grass, for a longer period than it can when following the scent of the animal's feet.

How can we put this knowledge about scent to the best use? First we must remember that the dog's knowledge will always be much greater than ours. If he appears at fault, he must not be blamed if conditions are very adverse.

The two principal uses for a dog on a rough shoot are to locate game or to find and retrieve game which has been shot. The first can be achieved on open ground by winding and pointing (or setting) and in thick cover by hunting and flushing. Retrieving will be either finding and bringing dead game, or hunting, finding and retrieving wounded game, ie runners. In order for a dog to carry out this mission effectively he must be fearless in thick cover and water alike.

On a day when scent is good a pointer may be allowed to range much more widely than when scent is bad. When it is bad he must be worked up-wind and the ground will have to be covered much more closely to avoid missing game. The same principles apply to a dog working in cover.

When scent is bad one may be forced to work the ground in the most favourable direction for the dog, even though tactically this is the worst direction, because it is towards the boundary. One is faced with the choice of losing birds over the march after they have been flushed, or not flushing them at all.

As far as retrieving dead or wounded game is concerned, if scent is poor then the dog should be sent out to retrieve as soon as is practical. If scent is good, a longer interval may be allowed. The worse the scent, the more important it is to mark the bird accurately. I remember an occasion when we were shooting grouse in beautiful, hot, sunny, October weather. The air was very warm and there was absolutely no scent at all. Two birds which I had marked roughly were sought by three different dogs. In the end, I picked both of them myself, the dogs having passed within a few yards on each occasion. Both birds were lying dead in heather with their plumage tightly folded and their heads to the wind. Had they been lying with the wind ruffling their feathers from behind, the dogs would have stood a much better chance. One of the guns who did not know my dog and who knew nothing about scent, said: 'Huh, your dog isn't much good is he?' In fact Bear was particularly good on grouse. So were the keeper's two dogs. With anything like good scenting conditions they would have winded both birds from not less than ten yards distance. I said nothing. I was perfectly satisfied that my dog, and the others, had done their best, under impossible conditions. That day we lost one bird within ten yards of a butt. The gun who had shot it had already trampled all over the ground, completely spoiling whatever scent there might have been.

Page 101 (*above*) A build up of geese will take place very quickly; (*below*) a labrador is the ideal dog for wildfowling

Page 102   My own personal choice is a labrador

8
Gathering Wounded Game

No sportsman likes to see any bird or beast wounded, and every possible effort must be made to recover any creature that has been wounded—or indeed any that are injured, or sick. For under conditions of modern life there are so many hazards, other than shooting, which cause injuries, or sickness. Many deer crossing roads at night are hit by vehicles. Usually the leader judges distance and speed accurately and will get across safely: it is one of the following deer that is more likely to be hit. Countless birds, game birds being no exception, are hit by motorists. Very large numbers of birds are killed or injured by telegraph or power lines. Often a bird flying into a power line will have its wing severed. It is said that 18 per cent of power failure is caused by mute swans colliding with power cables. Sickness may be caused by game birds picking up disease from domestic chickens—fowl pest, coccidiosis and gapes being most frequent. Rabbits may be sick with myxomatosis. These are some of the modern hazards which affect wildlife adversely, whilst oil is a terrible and devastating threat to wildfowl and other sea birds. Organo-chlorine pesticides and other chemicals have caused very serious loss of life or infertility in many species. It behoves everyone to avoid wasting life and also to put an end to suffering as speedily as possible. Motorists are often the most callous and cause much suffering; frequently it is the town driver who is responsible for running down a young brood of game birds, or bashing into a hen pheasant whose reactions are slowed down because she has just come off her nest or is heavy with eggs.

I learnt an excellent lesson about a wounded beast the very first time I was taken out shooting, as a very small boy. The ripe golden corn was being reaped by a binder pulled by a team of horses. There were many rabbits in the corn and I was allowed to stand beside my father as he shot those that bolted out towards the wood. The other gun was an uncle who was not a very expert shot—or so I thought then. At this distance in time I cannot remember many of the shots, but I remember as clearly as if it was yesterday one particular rabbit which ran out in front of my uncle. The rabbit seemed to flinch at each of his two shots and again at my father's single, long shot. Beyond the wheat field was a narrow grass field and then the oak wood beyond. I watched that rabbit all the way to the wood. It did not appear to run any more slowly than other rabbits, and yet I was so certain it had been hit that I expected to see it fall dead at any moment. My request to go to look for it was turned down.

The next day was a Sunday; I was very persistent in badgering my father to be allowed to go to look for that rabbit on Sunday morning, and at last, to my great delight, he gave way. The wood was farther from our house than I had ever been allowed to go alone, so it was an adventure to be allowed to go so far. I knew exactly where I had last seen that rabbit, just below a bush growing on the high bank which enclosed the wood, and at last I arrived at this bush. There was no rabbit. I was bitterly disappointed and wandered aimlessly along under the bank. Twelve or fifteen yeards farther I came upon the rabbit, stone dead, and stiff. But blood on its nose and a pellet hole or two through its ears proved without doubt that it was the very same rabbit. Its failing strength had caused it to turn from the steep bank and run along the base until death overcame it. I was very small at the time, and carrying that rabbit home was quite a task—but there was no happier boy in all Britain that morning, and my father's congratulations, and advice to watch every wounded bird or beast, as chance had led me to watch that rabbit, has never been forgotten. How well one remembers a simple lesson when one is at a most impressionable age!

There was another lesson to be learnt at my next shooting outing, a few months later. I was following my father along a ride through that same oak wood. His dog was working below the ride and suddenly what looked to my inexperienced eyes to be a very dark brown-black bird rose swiftly and flew fast down the ride. At his shot it fell dead just over the fence at the end of the ride. The gun was unloaded and carefully propped against a forked branch, where it could not fall. Then my father climbed the fence and picked the bird, which was a woodcock (why it had looked almost black to me I do not know. That only proves, what everyone knows who has to sift evidence from different people about the same incident, that people do not always see the same thing in an identical manner.) With childish enthusiasm I wanted to know why my father had not taken his gun with him. Surely there might have been something to shoot over the fence? But it was explained to me that the fence was the boundary, and that if a bird should fall over the boundary it was permissible to trespass in order to recover it, provided one's gun was left behind. After that I was shown the woodcock's 'pin' feathers at the 'bastard' joint of each wing and also how to draw the sinews out of the thighs by breaking and pulling the legs.

One more memory of woodcock must be related, because by chance it repeated both these first lessons. This was many years later when I was allowed to carry a gun. There was a large bracken-covered hill in Shropshire where I used to shoot rabbits. I got to know every portion of this hill like the back of my hand. There was usually one covey of French partridges there, but to a lone lad with a gun and a spaniel they were most elusive. There were five wet springs where a snipe could sometimes be found, and there were hundreds of rabbits. Always I hoped that one day I would come across a woodcock, but when, at last, it happened I was taken by surprise and my two shots were hopelessly ineffective.

Beyond me was a steep-sided valley with dense bracken on my side of the stream, and short cropped grass on the other side. I expected the woodcock to settle again in the bracken where I could walk it up and, being prepared, shoot it easily. But it flew on and on, and then, to my dismay, crossed the stream which was the boundary and swung back along the face of the opposite hillside. Sadly I watched it getting ever farther away—and then to my astonishment it crumpled, and fell dead, as though it had been shot by some unseen, ghostly gunner! It hit the ground and rolled over several times, so steep was the grassy slope. Leaving my gun at the boundary, I raced up that hillside and even today I can still recapture some of the feeling of intense delight as I gathered the warm bird and studied every detail of its beautiful plumage. One single pellet had brought about its downfall and given me my first woodcock. What a fortunate thing I had kept my eyes glued to it for so long!

Another incident comes to mind. I was outside gun of a line of guns walking up partridges. I fired at one of two partridges which crossed my front, and evidently missed. I watched them settle in the next field and run across the bare grass. Suddenly, whilst running, one of them collapsed and fell dead on its back. How many birds that are thought to be missed die unknown, their lives wasted! All the more reason to make every possible endeavour to search for, and gather, every bird or beast that is known to be wounded. Better by far to hold up the day's shoot for a while, and to gather one wounded bird, than to shoot three more. One of the joys of the rough shoot is that one can make time to look for a wounded bird more easily than one can on the large organised shoot—although on the big shoots the pickers-up and their dogs do not miss very much.

The following descriptions of the behaviour of wounded birds and beasts are given in the hope that this will enable others so wounded to be gathered.

A bird that is hit by a pellet, or pellets, from a shotgun will usually flinch, or check, sometimes almost imperceptibly, in flight. Often with an overhead or long side shot the pellets can be heard to strike; this is particularly the case with geese and other large birds. The sound is most often caused by the pellets striking the outstretched primary feathers of the wing, and it may well be that no pellet has struck the body. But if the bird has flinched it has been badly hit as well. It may carry on a long way before falling dead, or settling. If it settles the chances are that it will get up again, and it should be approached with caution and readiness. Any bird flying with a covey that separates after being shot at should be watched. The chances are that it is wounded and may be gathered when marked down. Game birds that are wounded may 'tower'. The bird flies up and up, sometimes to a great height, and dies at the peak of its flight, falling stone dead. Usually it is found to be lying on its back and often it is not so far away as it appears to be. It is a popular belief that the cause is a pellet in the lung. On rare occasions this may be so. But the usual reason is a simple internal haemorrhage within the body cavity, which causes giddiness, the bird raising its head to overcome this and automatically flying upwards as a result. Careful post-mortems will verify this fact.

I do not know why it is that 'towering' is confined almost entirely to game birds. I have seen several thousand geese and ducks shot, but I have never seen a goose, or a duck, or a pigeon perform a true tower, although I have heard of one or two cases and Patrick Chalmers in one of his delightful books wrote about a swan that towered. Curiously enough, the very first jack snipe that I ever shot towered. It flew a considerable distance to a great height and then fell dead into the middle of a huge bed of bracken; it was early October, before the bracken had gone down. I marked the spot as well as possible, and put a handkerchief down before I got to it and another well on the other side. I then went down on all fours, having no dog with me, and parted the bracken frond by frond until I found the bird. It was 140yd from where I shot at it! I have never seen another snipe tower.

A badly body-hit duck or goose (which might tower if it was a game bird) will fly with 'feathering' wingbeats, much less powerful than normal flight. Such a bird is worth watching for as long as it is in sight. Usually it will fall dead. A wounded pigeon may settle in a tree. Later, it is most likely to be found under the tree.

Sometimes a bird will make a 'false tower', rising not very

high, and then curving downwards, wings still beating. This indicates an injury to the head, often a skull injury. If the injury is superficial the bird may take off when approached. A bird which hovers or flies in a circle is hit in the eye. It may recover enough to fly a considerable distance and it is likely to get up again when approached. On rare occasions a bird may parachute down. Its wings remain spread, but motionless. Such a performance indicates a head wound, and very frequently the bird is stunned only. It may recover very quickly and fly clean away, so it should be approached with the gun at the ready. I have known several geese behave like this, and all needed to be shot again as they took off when approached.

A bird with a serious back injury, or both legs broken, will fly some distance in an erratic disjointed manner and then drop dead. A bird with one broken leg is not usually mortally injured and may well survive. However, obviously, every effort should be made to find it and finish it off.

A bird which has the tip of its wing damaged is bound to come down to the ground, but if flying high, down-wind, when wounded, it may go a long way. Pheasants, partridges, woodcock, ducks and geese will run when so wounded. A grouse and a pigeon may move a little distance, usually not far. A snipe will crouch and then try to take off when approached. It is a great mistake for a gun, or beater, or assistant, to try to pick a winged bird if a dog is available. Tramping around will destroy the scent for the dog, and if the ground cover is at all dense it is a hopeless task for a human to try to find a runner. It is often a mistake to try to guess which way it has gone. Often I have seen a dog called off a runner, because the owner thought it had gone in a different direction. Have faith in your dog and let him have his head: make quite sure that you are right, and he is wrong, before you recall him. Always give the dog the wind.

A winged duck, or goose, falling on land, will make for water if it is near by. But if it falls on water it will make for the bank as soon as it thinks it is safe to do so. It may be sound strategy to remain out of sight until the bird has had time to reach the shore.

It will make for rushes, or a rough bank with hiding-places. If your dog finds it, but fails to pick it at once, it will flap on the surface for a little way before it thinks of diving—and that is the best chance to finish it. Once it has started to dive, a long hunt may ensue, and a wounded duck lies so flat on water that it is by no means easy to finish it off with one shot. Always aim carefully at the head.

If a winged partridge is lost, it will often be found with the covey the next morning, when it may be picked easily.

Sometimes, after shooting at one of a skein of geese, I have seen the whole skein start to plane down to settle—and then suddenly flare up again. That means that a wounded goose has become the 'leader' as, dying, he slants down. When he hits the ground, dead, of course the others flare up in alarm. I have picked geese as much as three-quarters of a mile away by this means.

If a duck is retrieved in the dark, it may be difficult to tell whether it is dead. A dead duck's head hangs downwards, but a live duck will hold its head in a horizontal position. Many a duck has been lost after being retrieved and laid out for dead!

A wounded hare will travel a long way. If it has been seen to flinch at the shot, it may be gathered, dead, two or three hundred yards away.

Inexperienced sportsmen sometimes have difficulty in despatching a wounded bird or beast. Small game (grouse and partridges) can be tapped on the head. A wounded rabbit or hare should be picked up with the head held between the first and second fingers of one hand, the palm being uppermost. A quick downwards jerk results in the weight of the body dislocating the neck. Death is instantaneous and it can all be done with one hand, without putting down the gun. Geese are very difficult to kill. They should be held by the same two fingers and then the body must be rotated quickly. This dislocates the neck at once.

A deer that drops to a rifle shot should be treated as a wounded beast and approached at the ready. It may be stunned by the bullet hitting an antler or nicking one of the vertebrae and in that case it will recover and make off. A properly placed neck shot, or a bullet which cuts the arteries above the heart, will cause instant death, as will the severance of the spinal cord. But a normal heart shot (ie through the heart itself) will cause a very typical result: the beast will rush off with head stretched out and held low. Usually it will drop dead after 40–100yd. To a careful observer used to the gait of deer, this heart-shot gallop is quite distinctive. A deer shot in the lung may go some distance. The blood trail is pale and frothy. Dark blood means a heart or liver wound, flesh wounds producing blood of a less dark hue. It is therefore most important to note the exact position where a beast has been standing when the shot is taken. 'Pins' (hair) will denote a hit. 'Paint' (blood) will give an indication of the type of wound. A beast hit in the stomach moves in a tucked-up manner. It may go a long distance. Unless you know exactly where it is, so that it can be stalked and dispatched, or unless there is a dog handy to follow it, it should be given a considerable time to lie down and stiffen before it is followed up. Otherwise, if disturbed, it will draw on its reserve strength and may go a very great distance and be lost. Stags wounded during the rut are full of adrenalin and therefore have a greater resistance to wounds at this time. Sometimes a deer shot through the heart will turn into the wound a short distance before it drops. When this happens it will be found at a right-angle to the line of flight.

At any formal shoot it is of course the accepted rule that no one should carry a gun when picking-up. If there is reason to suppose that a wounded bird will get up again, permission to look for it with a loaded gun should be sought from the host or manager of the shoot. Obviously, great care must be taken to locate all beaters and other guns, for a wounded bird may fly in any direction. At any shoot where it is expected that a number of shots will be fired from one place it is advisable to have a back marker, preferably with a dog, to mark the position of wounded and dead birds. During a good duck flight the direction of departure of ducks that have been shot at should be noted, as frequently one or two can be picked the next day, a hundred yards or so away.

The whole subject of wounded game is a distressing one and every good sportsman will do all in his power to recover any wounded bird or beast as quickly as possible. However, it is my experience that a wounded creature either dies rapidly or recovers remarkably quickly. Indeed nature's power of recovery is astonishing.

But the one factor which causes more wounded game than any other is the taking of long shots. The stalker who boasts of killing a stag at 350yd only draws attention to his indifferent stalking ability and poor sportsmanship. The wildfowler who says he shot a goose stone dead at 80yd should not have raised his gun at all.

9
Vermin Control

It is a common concept nowadays that there is no such thing as vermin, other than perhaps bed bugs and fleas. It is fashionable to talk about 'predators', yet of all predators, anywhere, man is the most ruthless, selfish and devastating. Also, if one is to use the word predator in its most strict definition, then one must include a golden-crested wren eating a greenfly.

I prefer the good old-fashioned term of 'vermin'. Indeed it seems to me that ever since the 1954 Bird Act, and its subsequent amendments, the various winged vermin have become more easy to define. Those birds which are not protected (Schedule II), which affect game interests and which may be claimed as vermin, are carrion and hooded crow, magpie, jay, rook, jackdaw, greater and lesser black-backed gull and herring gull. In Argyll and Skye the raven is not protected. Birds which affect fishing interests and which are unprotected are cormorant, shag, and, in Scotland, goosander and merganser, these last two being protected in England and Wales.

All other birds are protected (other than some which have no impact upon game interests).

It is important to recognise the fact that all hawks and owls are protected by law. Buzzard, kestrel and the four owls, tawny, little, short-eared and long-eared, receive 'ordinary protection'. The remainder have 'special protection' (Schedule I). It is an offence to take or kill any of these species, or to take or destroy their eggs, at any time, except under special licence or under Section 4 (2) (a) of the 1954 Act.

In effect this section means that if action is taken to prevent serious damage to crops or other forms of property, including fisheries, it will be an acceptable defence in court if that action was necessary. But game species in the wild are not regarded as property, therefore this proviso affects shooting interests only when predators receiving ordinary protection are causing serious damage by taking game species which are not in a wild state. If 'specially protected' (Schedule I) predators are guilty of serious damage to game which are not in a wild state, then under Section 8 (1) (a) of the 1967 Act a licence to destroy the culprit(s) has to be obtained from the Home Office, for cases in England and Wales, or from the Secretary of State for Scotland. For killing Schedule I birds without a licence there are heavy penalties. (The appropriate legal language given in the Acts is longer and more precise than my summary, and of course it is this wording of the Acts which governs the legal position.)

It is obvious that there are many conflicting interests to be met. There is no doubt at all that eagles, hawks and owls are magnificent, spectacular and most interesting birds. It is also the case that, by and large, man's activities are having an adverse effect upon many of the species of these birds of prey. The most drastic damage has been caused by the use of pesticides which result in infertility or death. The shrinking of suitable habitat as a result of industrialisation and other human land uses, and the disturbance of nesting sites by hikers, tourists and sometimes by ornithologists, are also serious adverse factors. It is true that some protected predators are destroyed illegally on game preserves. It is not always realised that undue disturbance by bird-photographers and bird-watchers is also an offence.

It is true that a large proportion of the prey of these birds, when it consists of game birds, taken during the autumn and winter months, comes from the surplus stock of game or from weak birds and therefore is not a very significant loss. Those who advance this argument are apt to overlook the fact that it does not hold good, once game birds have taken up their territories and nesting sites. Predators still have to feed during the spring and summer, and every game bird, especially every female, killed during the breeding season is a serious loss. However, there is no legal redress for this loss, which must be accepted in the interests of conservation, which is especially important for those species whose future is in doubt. It is unfortunate that some protected species are rare, or non-existent, over the greater part of Britain, but common in certain limited areas, where habitat factors are favourable. Here the impact upon game may be heavy, and it is difficult for the local man, who knows only his own area, to realise that he may be in a key position as far as the future of a particular bird of prey is concerned.

Of the Schedule I (specially protected) birds, only golden eagles, peregrine, harriers, goshawk and sparrow-hawk are significant as far as harm to game interests is concerned. The golden eagle does take a few grouse and ptarmigan, many hares, and sometimes, perhaps, young lambs and deer calves; and surely he has a royal right to do so. The eagle is the greatest nuisance to shooting interests when a shooting party is lined out in the butts, with the beaters about to start, and he sweeps across the moor. The drive will be ruined, perhaps the whole morning spoilt, even the whole day. That is disappointing for the keepers who have worked all the year to provide the day's sport, and also to the guns who may have travelled some hundreds of miles. However, that, like the weather, is one of the hazards of grouse driving, and at least the stock of grouse is there for another day. The grouse keeper may dislike the eagle because of this; equally the stalker, wet and cold, crawling for the last few yards before his shot, will dislike the grouse that flushes in front of him and spoils his day!

The habitat of hen harriers often coincides with that of grouse and there is no doubt that a pair of harriers may take quite a number of grouse. This is just an unfortunate fact of life, which must be accepted. The montague harrier, even more rare, and the very scarce marsh harrier may have some slight impact on the rough shoot in East Anglia or the South of England.

The peregrine is a magnificent bird. The stoop of a peregrine is one of nature's most impressive sights. The kill is swift and clean and he is one of the true aristocrats of the air. Alas, the impact of toxic chemicals inside its prey has reduced this species from 700 pairs in Britain to 100 pairs, some of which are infertile as a result of poison. There has been some recovery in numbers recently. Grouse are immune from chemicals so it is the peregrines which feed on grouse which are also immune; other forms of prey are liable to be affected. It is most important to preserve peregrines. The goshawk is so rare in Britain that it need not concern us.

Last of the specially protected is the sparrow-hawk, the most recently added to the list. In the north this species is numerous, and my own view is that this hawk hardly merits ordinary protection. Certainly the impact of a sparrow-hawk upon partridges, where both species are present, is serious. In all too many areas where the partridge used to flourish, this grand little game bird has become extinct today, owing to changes in agricultural practice. The sparrow-hawk is one factor which influences the partridge's chance to make a comeback in marginal areas. This hawk is a ruthless and cruel killer. I have seen a hen sparrow-hawk eating a wood pigeon, which it had captured, but which was still alive. If a sparrow-hawk finds an easy prey, such as a covey of partridges, it will return day after day to search for survivors. Last winter a female discovered my tumbler pigeons, which numbered eleven. It took five in about a fortnight in spite of determined efforts to drive it away. Fortunately it met with a timely accident. But it is not everyone who has a room with a window at each end, on which an unpopular sparrow-hawk can bash its unwanted head.

The main case against the sparrow-hawk is that no one has ever taught it not to take other more attractive, rarer, Schedule I birds. In the rare-bird world, it is an anti-social delinquent. However, it is specially protected, and I, for one, deplore this.

Of those birds of prey on the ordinary protection list I propose to look at three species—the buzzard, the kestrel and the tawny owl. All are common.

I believe that most buzzards are reasonably well behaved, living on rabbits and voles. Once I knew of a pair in Wales that had learnt to live exclusively on homing pigeons, presumably caught when exhausted, on a particular fly line, through a pass in the hills. At any rate the nest was full of ringed domestic pigeon legs. This is exceptional. So was the pair that fed exclusively on chickens. These, when shot (long before the 1954 Act), were replaced by a normal pair of good behaviour. Buzzards do take young grouse, and if they get addicted to young grouse, which are easy to come by, they are a menace. There is no legal redress. But if they turn their addiction to pheasant poults in the release pen, they may be shot. It is not a frequent offence.

The tawny owl is a much more frequent offender with pheasant poults, with far more effect because he kills much more than he needs at any one time, storing the surplus in hollow trees and the like. When damage is serious the remedy lies under the provisions of Section 4 (2) (a) of the 1954 Act.

The kestrel is a very innocent and beautiful hawk. Just occasionally a delinquent will take to pheasant or partridge chicks on a rearing field in the first few weeks. But modern rearing is done in covered pens, so that the opportunity for a kestrel to misbehave should not be available.

I have dealt with those species which it is not permitted to kill (with certain defined exceptions) at some length. It is essential for the amateur keeper to understand the legal position. Above all there is a great need for tolerance: tolerance on the part of the shooting man towards the conservationist (fortunately most true sportsmen are also very keen on conservation) and tolerance towards sportsmen on the part of those whose task is the difficult one of conserving wildlife. It is deplorable that there is a tendency to blacken the reputation of all gamekeepers, and many shooting men, simply because a few have disregarded the law. Who is in a better position to look after the welfare of rare birds than the keeper who knows every inch of the ground? It is better to seek his co-operation, which is often freely available, than to treat him as an ignorant blackguard.

Now I must turn to winged vermin which are not protected. It is illegal to use spring traps of any design, poison or stupefying substances, nets, snares, hooks, electricity or gas, or mechanically propelled vehicles. That does not leave very much: cage traps, shooting and the destruction of nests and eggs about sums it up. Incidentally, if my reading of the Act is correct, a motorist who runs over and kills a specially protected (Schedule I) bird could incur a £25 fine and/or imprisonment for a first offence.

Shooting is efficient as a measure of control, but it is rarely effective in eliminating unwanted vermin. All too often the surplus population is destroyed, with a small proportion of the hard-core breeding stock, but far too many crows and gulls learn the range of a gun very quickly, and escape.

Formerly, the most efficient method of control was by the use of strychnine, which is legal only for poisoning moles, and phosphorus-based poisons inserted into an egg, dead rabbit or other similar bait. By this means hoodie and carrion crows and magpies could be eliminated. But strychnine is indestructible. Whatever eats the victim will die, and whatever eats that will also die. Phosgene is very rapid. Both are dangerous to handle, and their use is illegal. A substitute is urgently required. Alpha chlorolose is very effective and its action is confined normally to the first victim. The best antidote is a spell in the airing cupboard or some other very warm corner. It has been widely used, illegally. The dose of this substance can be adjusted so as to stupefy or kill the victim, according to the size of the dose and the weight of the victim. There is a very urgent need to legalise the controlled use of this, or some similar substance, so that the Corvidae and big gulls can be dealt with efficiently. Perhaps we need a Doped Egg Marketing Board!

What steps can the owner of a rough shoot take? First, he should put out crow traps. These are cages approximately 6ft square and the same height, made of 2in wire netting. In the centre of the top a funnel should be inserted about 4ft in diameter, tapering to 2ft 6in diameter at 2ft from the ground. Perches should be arranged inside the cage well above the level of the bottom of the funnel. A well-fitting door for human access for baiting and for dealing with crows which are caught must be included. The door should be fitted with a padlock. A bowl of water should be available inside the cage. A catching-net on the principle of a fisherman's landing-net is required for dealing with the catch. It is sometimes an advantage to have a funnel at ground level and I have heard of one such cage trap which was found to hold a crow, a buzzard and a wild cat at the same time! Where cattle are present, the cage must be protected by a barbed-wire surround.

The best bait to use is carrion in the form of dead animals, or fish or eggs. Stale bread is quite attractive, too. The most effective time to use cage traps is January, February and March, especially during hard weather. It is essential to pre-bait the cage, with the door open, until numbers of crows have learnt to use the cage. Then the trap should be set later in the evening. After a good catch has been made it is best to rest the trap and to concentrate for a period on another, elsewhere—or to move the trap if it is sectional, which is an advantage. An adult male crow, if left in the trap (with food, water, and shelter), may attract others. One that calls frequently is the most effective. The same cage is suitable for rooks, and a sheep-netting top avoids the need for a funnel.

The siting of a cage trap is important. A little distance from an isolated tree or small clump of trees used by crows as a vantage-point is an effective site.

Apart from cage traps, an all-out war on the Corvidae is required by shooting. Hoodie and carrion crows, and magpies, have winter roosts, as of course have rooks and jackdaws (and sometimes ravens). Some can be shot on their way to roost and many can be shot at the roost from a well-sited, well-camouflaged hide. But this method will only reduce the numbers, not eliminate them.

Crows and magpies can be decoyed to a stuffed owl or stuffed cat, although how you stuff an owl without killing it illegally I am not certain.

During the winter every old nest of crow and magpie should be noted, and a very keen eye should be kept for new nest-building in the spring. A magpie will sit very tight. Ideally two

Page 119 (*above*) A good working spaniel; (*below*) gathering wounded game

Page 120 (*left*) The art of ferreting;
(*below*) for the beginner—the woodpigeon

guns should approach from opposite sides and it may take quite a lot of stone-throwing to flush the bird off the nest. If she is missed then she will not be so accommodating the second time. It is a mistake to fire a shot at the nest. The mud lining is so thick, and a magpie's body so small, that it is rare to obtain a kill. I have climbed up to a magpie's nest after a number of shots had been fired, only to find the young unharmed. It is better to poke out the nest, but this is a confession of failure, as it is the old birds that one wants to kill, before the young hatch.

Hoodie and carrion crows cannot be approached until they are sitting tight at the end of at least one week. Even then they may slip away out of shot. It may be necessary to construct a hide near the nest from which to shoot. It is essential to have a companion who can walk away from the hide after one is concealed, as the bird will then think that the hide is not occupied. Jackdaws can be shot as they leave their nests in hollow trees. A ·22 rifle is an excellent weapon for destroying crows or black-backed gulls, although these birds get wise to it quickly.

The other major type of vermin is ground vermin. In most of Scotland and parts of Wales, where there is no hunting interest, the fox, a most efficient predator, must be destroyed. Where hunting interests are paramount, it is most important to establish the fullest co-operation between the shooting and hunting folk of the countryside. The shooting estate must be able to show a fox when hounds meet. The effect of hounds drawing a covert, or running through, is negligible on a stock of hand-reared pheasants. But it is unrealistic to say that foxes do no harm to game at all, and it is up to the master to make a special effort to deal with foxes where they are doing a lot of damage.

In hill country it may be necessary to kill foxes for the sake of the lambs. Foxes are almost omnivorous, eating fruit and flesh alike; voles, rabbits, bilberries and blackberries in season, and frogs, are all much sought. It is when foxes take the hen pheasant, partridge or grouse off the nest that they do the worst harm. This happens most at hatching time, when the sitting hen shuffles about and gives off more scent. A fox in a pheasant laying pen, or at the release pen, can do untold harm, as he will kill and bury far more than he requires to eat.

It is illegal to use gin traps for foxes or to use poison, and although they may still be snared this is a bad method of control because roe are caught all too frequently. A fox snare should have a stop to prevent it running too tight.

The main method of attack is via the earths, or dens as they are called in Scotland. Often the local shepherd knows where the traditional earths are situated. They can be bolted by terriers; or it is possible to wait for foxes to come out in the evening, or return at dawn, and shoot them. Obviously the wind must be right and complete freedom from movement or noise is necessary.

A very efficient method is to construct warm artificial earths which can be visited from time to time. Driving thick plantations to guns strategically posted is another method, but it is necessary to have very reliable shots who know what they are doing.

In many parts of Scotland, the wild cat is not the rare animal it is reputed to be. Where it occurs at all, it is numerous—often more numerous than foxes. It is a cunning, efficient, vicious killer of game, rabbits, hares and roe deer kids, operating at night and in the evening and early morning. Wild cats are easy to trap —much more so than foxes. A trap placed on a pole over a stream was most effective when it was legal.

The domestic cat gone wild is also a ruthless predator, although it is not as efficient as its wild cousin. Both can be trapped in cage traps. A rabbit or a kipper make a suitable bait and a 'drag' trail should be made leading to the trap. A dog will 'tree' a cat, when it may be shot. A terrier will bolt a wild cat from its den, but there is some risk to the terrier.

Tracks of cats and foxes should be sought in the snow and on sandy roads or muddy banks of streams. A dog fox has his 'lamp posts' which he visits at regular intervals to cock his leg, thus registering his presence, just as a dog does. Both a fox and a cat are regular in their habits, the fox more so than the cat.

People often say 'what bad luck, the one night I forgot to shut up my hens, a fox came and killed them'. That is not coincidence. The fox has his regular round.

The remaining animals which need control to prevent predation are mink, stoats, weasels, grey squirrels and rats, and perhaps polecats where they are numerous. Of all these animals, the rat is the most destructive, but mink are the most vicious killers.

A plentiful supply of tunnels set with a Fenn trap inside (unbaited) and visited regularly will take a heavy toll of all these species. Old banks, gaps in hedgerows, planks over ditches and so forth make suitable places. A day spent with an experienced keeper going round his tunnel traps is never wasted. A Fenn trap set in a hole baited with a dead rabbit will catch stoats.

Warfarin is a lethal method of eliminating rats except in those areas when they have become immune. It is now legal to use Warfarin for grey squirrels, if placed in suitable tunnels, and alpha chlorolose for Warfarin-resistant rats. It can be obtained from the Cambrian Chemical Farm Ltd, Beddington Farm Road, Croydon, CR0 4XB.

I have not mentioned otters or badgers. Otters should not be killed. Occasionally Brock will turn rogue and become a killer of chickens and penned game birds. When this happens he should be dealt with as speedily as possible, in his own interest, for he will be found to be suffering from an injury—loss of teeth, an injured leg or general debility due to old age. However, since early 1974 badgers have been given full protection by law.

Of all the vermin species, the most important to deal with, by all possible methods, are crows, magpies, rats, foxes in non-hunting country, and cats.

10
The Young Shot: Squirrels, Rabbits, Hares, Pigeons

A rough shoot is the ideal training-ground for a young lad—after he has been schooled thoroughly in the safe and proper handling of a gun. Safety lessons should begin long before he handles a gun at all. Thus it is very beneficial for a young sportsman, before he uses a gun himself, to accompany his father, or an experienced shot, on as many outings as possible. On such occasions proper shooting etiquette should be explained to him. He will also have an opportunity to learn much about the habits and behaviour of game and wildlife in general. In short, let him become a good countryman before he is allowed to handle a gun.

When the time comes for him to be taught to use a gun, one of the first lessons, which should be demonstrated to all beginners, is to impress upon him the devastation which a shotgun causes, when fired at close quarters. Let him place an empty cartridge carton on bare soil, with a safe background, and let a shot be fired at this at 10yd range. The resulting hole in the ground should be impressed upon his memory for all time, for even a high-powered rifle is scarcely more devastating than a charge of No 6s at very close range.

Most sportsmen of the older generation, who have done a lot of shooting, are partially deaf. I have lost the joy of listening to the song of many of our most melodious songbirds. In fact, when this first happened, I thought that suddenly chiffchaffs had become excessively rare, and it was a couple of years before I discovered the wretched truth that I could no longer hear them. Today there is no reason for anyone to suffer from shooting deafness.

Very efficient ear plugs can be obtained and there is no doubt at all that every youth should avail himself of this protection. Apart from the fact that it is a nuisance not to be able to hear well what other humans are saying, it is a grave handicap for a sportsman not to be able to hear the tiny woodland sounds which mean so much. It is also very frustrating to see a wren, that charming and most ubiquitous bird, sitting near by, with its beak working overtime—and not one sound being uttered. I have had this experience when waiting motionless in a duck hide, whilst a wren, unaware of my presence, sat on a corner post of the hide and sang for all the world—except me—to hear. So, let ear plugs be the order of the day for all those who are commencing their shooting career.

A very early test, which every beginner must make, is to ascertain which is his master eye. It is perfectly simple to find out. With both eyes open the index finger of one hand should be pointed at any stationary object. If the left eye is then shut and the finger remains pointing at the object, then his right eye is master and he should learn to shoot from the right shoulder. If his finger appears way out to the left of the object, then his left eye is master, as can be proved by lining up the finger again and shutting the right eye—when the finger will still be aligned as with both eyes open. If that is the case it is better to learn to shoot from the left shoulder than to use a cross-eyed stock from the right shoulder.

Most experienced shots will agree that the most important single factor that goes to make a good shot is correct gun mounting. Therefore it is far better to be coached by a professional coach at a shooting school than to be taught only the principles of safety and then be turned out into the shooting field. Bad habits in gun mounting are easily acquired and much less easily corrected afterwards. Let every beginner be trained properly from the start.

It is also very important to use a gun which fits. But the best-fitting gun in the world will not provide good shooting unless it is handled and mounted properly.

I will not presume to try to put on paper instructions which are far better instilled on the shooting ground, except to say that the most simple (of very many) techniques is usually the most efficient. My father's advice to me was: 'Learn to pick your bird [out of a covey] quickly, concentrate on that bird and shoot straight at it.' It was some years later that I began to worry about 'lead' and 'forward allowance', with ill effects upon my standard of shooting.

Major John Ruffer's advice, equally simple, but more precise, is devastatingly effective: 'Mount with the muzzle pointing at the bird all the way and fire as the gun touches the shoulder.' I have found that this works with the tallest geese and the tallest pheasants, without any conscious lead, as long as I remember to do it! If one watches a first-class shot performing, he does just this with a smooth and apparently unhurried movement, which makes it look so easy.

Anyway, we will assume that the young shot has been properly schooled in all safety measures, and in the proper handling and mounting of his gun, before he reaches the rough shoot. He must also know that if he has the misfortune of an off day, and shoots badly, his host will be understanding. But if he does not handle his gun safely (100 per cent safely) all day, his host may send him home forthwith, and certainly neither his host, nor other guests present, will ever again invite him to shoot. Next to an unsafe shot, the most objectionable guest is the greedy, selfish shot.

The rough shoot will provide the young shot with the two things he most needs at the start of his shooting career. The first and most important item is fieldcraft. If he has an inquiring mind and an observant eye he will discover that half the pleasure of shooting is to learn the habits of his quarry and to try to discover the reasons behind any particular reactions and inter-relationships of wildlife. Much he will learn from the experience of his older companions, but the best knowledge comes from personal experience. The second item is practice with the gun. Because game birds are not always very numerous on a rough shoot, he may have to turn his attention to grey squirrels, rabbits or pigeons, all of which are worthy adversaries, especially if stalked.

Grey squirrels concentrate on beech mast and acorns in the autumn in a mast year, as do wood pigeons. Squirrels also eat sweet chestnuts and the seeds in pine cones, Scots pine and Corsican pine being preferred, stripping off the hard scales and dropping them to the ground. After all the seeds are eaten, the central stem of the cone is stripped bare, and then it is discarded too. Crossbills, which also eat the seed, do not tear off the scales. They prise them open with their powerful beaks and then drop the whole cone with the shredded scales still in place. Greater spotted woodpeckers eat pine seeds too. But they fix the cone in a crevice in the bark of a tree and then extract the seed. Sometimes quite a heap of woodpecker cones may be found in one place.

So, if one comes across the scales scattered on the forest floor under a pine tree, with the stem of the cone, that is a sure sign that one or two squirrels are feeding in that tree. A very stealthy stalk at about eight o'clock the next morning may provide a shot at the culprit. There is no better way for a young man to learn the art of stalking. If he proceeds slowly and carefully he will see the scales falling to the ground and that will indicate the position of the squirrel. He still has to get within shot without disturbing the squirrel.

In late winter or early spring good sport may be had by poking nests or dreys with long aluminium rods made for the purpose. (The same rods are useful for 'lofting' decoy pigeons.) Ideally it needs a party of four. One person does the poking, two guns or one gun and one ·22 rifle stand each side of the tree, and the third gun follows up 300yd behind. It is the third gun or rifle who accounts for squirrels which have escaped by lying doggo, as these squirrels move when the front party leaves the area. Squirrel-poking days should not start too early. Time must be allowed for the squirrels to return to their dreys, where they spend the day after their morning feed. They will not be found at home late in the afternoon either, as by then they will be out feeding again.

Where squirrels are numerous in hardwood forests, seventy or eighty may be shot by this means in one outing. Grey squirrels are very destructive to pole crops of beech, sycamore and oak. They eat the bark during the late spring, thus killing or mutilating the crop. So it is most important to try to eliminate the squirrel population in or near vulnerable tree crops, before damage occurs.

There are still many areas in Britain where rabbits have not recovered from myxomatosis. But there are also areas where the numbers are back to pre-myxi levels, because the disease no longer has the same lethal virulence that it had in 1954.

In such areas rough-shoot rabbits are splendid training for the young sportsman. My first three shots on my first outing with a 12-bore were at two rabbits and a wood pigeon, all stalked with infinite patience and all shot sitting! What anguish of dismay there was when the very first one dived down its hole at my shot—and what delight when I found that it was stone dead just inside the hole! What excitement when a pigeon settled in a tall pine tree: to get within shot seemed hopeless, but, moving very slowly and cautiously, and almost breathlessly, from tree to tree, I narrowed the distance. At last I was under the Scots pine and there was the pigeon right above me, its gaze on some distant object. The gun was raised very slowly, the trigger squeezed and the unfortunate pigeon plummeted to the ground—and one small boy could scarcely believe his good fortune.

Stalking rabbits in a late summer's evening or early in the morning, with a ·22, is good sport. Walking them up in winter with a shotgun is excellent sport. But to my mind the best sport of all is obtained by ferreting, and although there is a tendency for modern rabbits to live underground rather less than their forebears, there are good warrens to be found wherever rabbits have made a comeback. The art of ferreting is less likely to be understood today than formerly. There are fewer good ferrets about, too.

Many people dislike ferrets: 'nasty, stinking things—you can't trust them'. A ferret is a clean animal, and it stinks only if it is kept in unclean conditions. Ferrets should be handled when quite young, and once a human being has gained their confidence by frequent handling and kindness, they are perfectly trustworthy. In fact they make delightful pets. As a youth I had a huge male or hob polecat ferret that would follow me like a dog for long distances. He would come to the whistle and I could pick him up by his front paws without his attempting to bite. Just as a shooting dog requires training, so does a ferret, although the training of a ferret is simpler. As with other animals, humans included, ferrets should never be over-fed. If they are kept in good condition and fit there is no need to starve them before a day's work. In fact a starved ferret is more likely to kill underground and then lie up after making a big meal.

When ferreting one must make a silent and careful approach to the warren. Never approach down-wind. The two guns should take up position in complete silence, one each side of the warren. Do not allow your dog to gallop about blowing down each hole. Tread lightly when approaching a hole to put in the ferret. When a rabbit appears at the mouth of a hole, remain absolutely motionless and, above all, make no attempt to shoot it. Many a good ferret has been shot because it is close behind the rabbit. Let the rabbit break clear before it is shot. It is important that a wounded rabbit should be finished off before it gets down a hole again, or it will cause a lay-up and delay the day's sport.

Ferreting is great sport so long as the rabbits bolt well. It is very exciting to hear them rumbling and thumping underground. Often there are special bolt-holes—small round holes half-concealed, because they are excavated from within, without any tell-tale spoil at the entrance. Rabbits bolt from these very fast and often take one by surprise.

A fisherman can often predict when trout will be rising and a good rabbiter can forecast when conditions are right for rabbits to bolt. But both may be proved wrong. Rabbits bolt well on a clear, crisp frosty morning. On the other hand, under such conditions, vibrations from careless footsteps, or from any sound, will be heard by the rabbits more freely, and then they may not bolt. A wet, rainy day is often disappointing, but on a rough windy day I have known them bolt well: probably the factor then is the simple one that they are unaware of human presence.

When a ferret does not show up it is because it has either killed and is lying up, or has cornered a rabbit in a dead-end hole and cannot make it move. An experienced rabbiting dog will frequently be able to locate the exact position of the ferret. By placing an ear to the ground, one may be able to hear the ferret, especially if it is working to get at a rabbit at a dead end. If that happens, it will have fur in its claws when it comes out. A reliable line ferret, worked on a collar and ferret line, may cause the original ferret to move. If the line ferret lies up too, it is a fairly simple matter to dig to its position, using the line as a guide. A long briar pushed up the hole may dislodge the ferret and, if skilfully twisted into the fur of a dead rabbit, may be used to draw it out.

If all else fails, paper or bracken lighted at the mouth of a hole, so that the smoke permeates through the warren, will often cause a ferret to come out. Generally speaking, the more ferrets are used and handled, the less they lie up. A shy ferret, which comes to the mouth of the hole and then retreats as soon as an attempt is made to pick it up, is an abomination. It is in the same category as an untrained dog.

Where rabbits have got out of hand, every possible means must be used to eliminate them. The warrener who turns in the most rabbits is not necessarily the most efficient. It is easy to cream a large number of rabbits off a large area, but such a method has little influence on the total population—other than keeping it healthy. It is better to work systematically over an area, using all practical means, and not move to the next block until the last is clear. Snaring with a minimum of 300 snares is efficient for a start. But the most efficient method of elimination is by cymag, a substance placed inside the holes to give off poisonous fumes. Shooting is the least efficient method, but the most sporting.

Good sport can be had shooting rabbits at harvest time. The guns must stand close up to the standing corn and they must shoot outwards. Similarly, when shooting driven rabbits crossing a ride, in contrast to game shooting, the guns must stand with their backs to the cover being driven, shooting the rabbits after they have passed. This is an elementary safety precaution. (The same principle applies to the magnificent sport of shooting wild boar on the Continent with a rifle *en battue*.)

In many parts of the country hare shoots are arranged after the game season is over. A hare shoot is not necessarily the best schooling for a young shot, because it involves a large number of guns, some of whom take out a gun only on this special annual occasion, and not all those present are perfectionists in the matter of correct and safe gun handling. As about half the guns act as armed beaters, and the other half as forward guns, there is a need for stringent safety measures, and indeed most who take part are perfectly safe.

There are several tips for the young shot to observe at a hare shoot. The first is never to fire long shots. It is very easy to wound a hare, and a wounded hare is a pitiful sight. Hares are large animals and I prefer to use No 4s rather than smaller sized shot. If one is a walking gun it is necessary to curb one's enthusiasm. Nobody else is going to carry the hares which one has shot. If one is a standing gun, one must make one's own decision as to whether it is safe to shoot in front. At a blue hare shoot the ground is often strewn with rocks and boulders and the danger of a possible ricochet off a rock must be considered.

Hares do not very clearly see objects which are directly in front of them, unless there is some movement to catch their eye. Therefore it is important to remain motionless when a hare is approaching. In fact, this is a lesson which a young shot must learn early in his career. The gun (or rifle) who can master the art of immobility will have more shooting than his fidgety neighbour. This truth applies to any quarry, from deer crossing a woodland glade beyond a waiting rifle to rats creeping out from a corn rick. In order to remain still it is necessary to dispose one's limbs in a reasonably comfortable position: to relax one's body, but to remain fully alert mentally.

Blue hares (which are white in winter), are much less wary than brown hares. They are rather stupid and much softer and more easily killed. In some areas as many as a thousand may be shot in one day.

Before myxomatosis, it was unusual for brown hares to be numerous on land which was heavily infested with rabbits. Apart from competition over food, I believe that rabbits infected hares with disease, although hares are immune from myxomatosis, or almost completely so. Since rabbits have come back, I have noticed that hares and rabbits share the same ground more than they used to before.

Another universal quarry for the beginner is the wood pigeon. In Britain the following pigeons and doves are found.

The wood pigeon, ring dove or cushat as it is called (or just plain 'doo' in Scotland), is the most numerous. It is also the largest, distinguished by a white wing patch on the wing and by a white patch, with green and purple, on the side of the neck. This patch is missing from juveniles, which may cause confusion. I well remember how I shot my first juvenile (I was also pretty juvenile) as it flew out of a holly bush. I thought I had secured a very rare variation and sent it away to be stuffed. In fact it was already stuffed with a great number of holly berries! Unlike most birds other than pigeons, the main breeding season is from July to the end of September.

The stock dove is much smaller than the wood pigeon. It has no white on the neck or on the wings which have two short black bars. It breeds in holes in trees and sometimes in rabbit holes in sand dunes, and flies with much faster wingbeats than does the wood pigeon. It is rare in the north of Scotland and absent from Caithness.

The rock pigeon, a cliff-breeder, is similar to the stock dove, except that it has a very marked white rump and its plumage is more blue than grey. The pure rock dove is rather rare, since it interbreeds freely with feral domestic pigeons. Indeed, most domestic pigeons originated from rock doves. Feral pigeons are very common on cliffs and around derelict buildings.

There are two true doves. The turtle dove, a summer migrant, does not breed in Scotland, Ireland or West Wales. It is protected.

The collared dove, a smoky-grey bird, first reached southern Britain in 1952. By 1957 it had nested in Morayshire. Today it is common in villages and suburbs from the Shetlands to the Scilly Isles. It is not really a country bird, living on the fringes of towns, hamlets and villages. It is not protected in Scotland, but is still protected in England.

Of all these species it is the wood pigeon and stock dove which will be the main quarry for the young pigeon shooter, but it is necessary for him to distinguish the other species and it is absolutely essential that he should distinguish the flight of domestic pigeons from wood pigeons, because it is a grave offence to shoot a homing or racing pigeon or any domestic pigeon. Therefore, feral domestic pigeons should be shot only when it is certain beyond any doubt that they are feral.

Broadly speaking, there are three main methods of shooting pigeons. They can be shot coming in to roost, intercepted during passage between the roost and the feeding area, or decoyed on their feeding grounds.

Shooting at the roost can be quite productive within certain limits. It needs proper planning. Often, after the game season, there are organised pigeon days when many guns turn out to cover a large number of roosts, and in theory this should work well. In practice I do not believe it is very productive of large bags. There are two reasons for this. Unless there is rough weather, a large number of pigeons will be disturbed over a very wide area, but only a small number will be shot at and many of those will be too high. The other reason is that there is no prior preparation. George and Bill are sent to one wood, John to another and Frank to a third. None may know the ground intimately and it is unlikely that proper hides have been built. Therefore they are shooting under a great handicap and dispersing the pigeons unnecessarily.

As with all forms of shooting, the precise position chosen for each gun is of the greatest importance. It is necessary to fulfil three requirements. First, the gun must cover a main flight line into, or within, the wood. Second, he must have enough overhead space to shoot effectively. Third, he must be well concealed, and that means a well-placed, well-camouflaged hide. Success depends upon the gun coming up to the shoulder before the pigeon sees the shooter: it should then be a dead bird that never knew what hit it. The best bags are made at pigeons which come in boldly, and that presupposes that they have not been shot at in that roost recently, that there is a strong wind, and that the guns are well-placed and properly concealed.

After a roost has been shot up, most of the pigeons will go elsewhere, and those that return will be very shy for a fortnight or so.

Therefore it could be argued that rather than disturb every wood on one night it is better to make a concentrated attack on the main roosts on different nights, choosing rough weather and using carefully sited hides. Be that as it may, if some decoys can be lofted on to the tops of bare winter branches near the hide, that is often a great advantage, provided the would-be shooter does not waste half the shooting time trying to get his decoys lofted, or stun himself by dropping a wooden decoy on to his own head, both of which events I have known to happen.

There are very many pigeon roost woods where an elevated high stand can be of enormous advantage. It is tremendous fun to shoot pigeons coming, like driven grouse, at eye level, from a hide placed in the top of a tree. Stability, proper camouflage and plenty of shooting space are the main essentials. Sometimes a high seat used for shooting deer by rifle can be adapted for use as a high pigeon hide.

The second method of shooting pigeons, that is on passage between the roost and the feeding grounds, requires very detailed knowledge of pigeon movements. It has the great merit of not disturbing roost or feeding ground, and therefore it can be done more frequently from the same place.

I knew a wood in Wales which was a roost for huge numbers of pigeons. On the down-wind side of the wood there was a long, steep, scrub-covered bank, and the pigeons flew along the contours of this slope on their way to the wood. I built three hides straight across the contours, and when there was a strong south-westerly three of us would be certain of a terrific shoot, firing as fast as we could reload. The wood was preserved as a sanctuary and therefore there was always a good flight coming into the wood. There are many places where a similar policy would pay off much better than shooting within the roost wood.

Decoying pigeons on their feeding ground is the most productive form of pigeon shooting. But it requires adequate preparation, and a knowledge of pigeon feeding habits. Taking the calendar as a guide, snowy weather in January or February will see pigeons concentrating, often in great numbers, on fields of kale, rape, and, when they are grown as field crops, sprouts and cabbages. During mild open weather in early spring they will feed on clover leys, eating the buds and young clover shoots. As soon as the spring sowing takes place they will concentrate on newly sown fields, peas being a certain draw. Throughout the early summer pigeons are more widely dispersed over the countryside, often feeding on pastures. In hill country, in July, where there are bilberries, good sport may be had at pigeons coming to the berries. But as soon as the corn begins to ripen, they will take to it greedily. Wheat and barley are preferred to oats. Again, peas are a favourite attraction. Where corn has been laid, the pigeons will concentrate as soon as it begins to ripen.

After harvest, there is the acorn crop and beech mast and then there are sowings of winter wheat, clover leys, ivy and holly berries and, finally, with hard weather, kale and brassicas.

So the would-be pigeon shooter must spend some time travelling around with a pair of field glasses just watching to find out where the pigeons are feeding. In fact he should know the fields that are likely to draw pigeons before the conditions are right for them to use those fields.

Having found the places where the pigeons are feeding, it is still desirable to spend an hour or more watching, and planning, for an onslaught the next day. The exact position for the hide must be chosen with care, in relation to the wind direction, the most suitable cover, the best place for putting up the decoys and the general direction from which the pigeons are flighting. Pigeons will always have one or two special look-out points to which many of them fly before dropping down to feed. A hide 40 or 50yd down-wind of such a look-out position, which is usually an isolated or tall tree, will be very effective. But it is important not to set up one's hide where the bulk of the shot pigeons will fall into standing corn.

I prefer a sitting hide, and that means that a hole must be dug for my legs, as one cannot crouch uncomfortably for long. Where possible, I like to place my decoys so that the pigeons, which will come in up-wind, cross my front.

A large number of decoys (say twenty) is desirable. To these should be added those shot, from time to time. A forked stick will hold up the head, or a pointed stick inserted through the mouth and out through the crop will do the trick. However, too much time need not be wasted on this. As long as some decoys are properly set, a mass of blue corpses dispersed with their heads down will still attract pigeons—the more the better. Even dead pigeons lying upside down, or clumps of feathers, do not put off newcomers, provided the bulk of the decoys are placed properly. In warm weather, bluebottles will soon find the dead pigeons, so it is important to carry a fly spray to prevent the dead birds becoming fly-blown. It is a fallacy to place every decoy heading into the wind. Nothing could look more unnatural than a set of decoys arranged with complete symmetry and spaced with mathematical precision.

Good decoys can be bought from many reliable sources. But for those who like to make their own, any old car tyre will make eight, although cutting them out is tedious. They are curved in exactly the right shape and they fit one into the other. They need to be painted with a matt paint.

The controversy about the best size of shot for shooting pigeons is an old one. I do not know why there should be any doubt. A plucked pigeon is a small bird and small birds need a dense pattern which is provided by small shot. Many pigeons appear to be mortally wounded because a puff of feathers comes out at the shot. But pigeons have a great number of feathers and they are dislodged so easily that this does not necessarily mean a mortal wound. I have proved to my own satisfaction that No 7s give far better results and leave far fewer wounded pigeons than No 4s.

Anyway, the sport of shooting pigeons will provide the young shot with food for much thought and a great deal of experience and endless pleasure. But the main consideration of all must be for the interests of the farmer. No crops must be damaged, gates must not be left open, cars must not be left where they will block farm machinery and, needless to say, permission must always be obtained before any private land is entered, or a shot fired.

11
Equipment and Camouflage

So much of the pleasure of shooting lies in preparation and planning. So much of the success depends upon sensible equipment, and this is where the modern sportsman has a great advantage over the older generations, because there is such a wealth of good equipment available today: perhaps too much.

Light green rubber knee boots and thigh boots are so light that one hardly knows one has them on. I have stalked all day in light thigh boots, without feeling at all tired. Bamas worn inside absorb all moisture, and electric boot driers dry out one's boots efficiently after one has gone over the top. Kammo wear disguises the rough shooter and there are many other excellent types of shooting jackets, waterproofs and headgear. I prefer a Barbour Thornproof for outer wear and I find a deerstalker-type hat preferable to all others for the simple reasons that it covers the upper part of my face and keeps the rain from dripping down my neck. Incidentally, the human face resembles nothing else in nature other than a turnip. Unless disguised, it is a warning to most wild creatures. Therefore a face mask is essential for wildfowl or pigeon shooting, and useful for deer. So there is no longer any need to smear one's face with mud, or burnt cork, Many people shoot in trousers nowadays. The old-fashioned knickerbockers or plus fours are preferable. On a wet day, the rain collects round the overhang and drains off readily. Trousers or riding breeches become clammy when wet.

A waterproof skirt, worn over one's trousers, like a kilt, is the most efficient wildfowling equipment for wet weather and muddy places. When standing, it prevents water from running down the inside of one's thigh boots, and one can sit down on damp ground and still maintain a dry bottom—and why should ladies and the Scots have a monopoly of this particular type of garment?

In fact, comfort in clothing is one of the secrets of keeping warm for long periods of waiting. The alternative to a waterproof skirt is waterproof shorts. But they tend to ruck up above the top of thigh boots, because few standard types are long enough. Full-length waterproof trousers are too long to wear over thigh boots, but ideal over gum boots, except that one cannot see the plimsoll line when walking near the limit.

There are many types of shooting jacket on the market. Provided it is roomy enough not to cramp one's mounting of the gun, is of a suitable colour and not shiny (as are some waterproofs) and is fitted with large side pockets and a hare pocket, the exact pattern is a matter of personal choice. If it is fitted with a smart belt, throw that away. Nothing restricts shoulder movement and natural swing more.

For woodland deer stalking the very best clothing is a loden mantle (or cloak) or a full-length loden coat, as is used universally on the Continent. This material is made out of mohair and it is as soundless as a deer's coat, when moving through undergrowth. It is warm, light and completely waterproof. I do not know why this first-class material has never become popular amongst British sportsmen.

There is a wider choice in guns today than ever before. For the young lad a 20-bore is the best starter. He will never want to part with it in later life. When he is of sufficient stature let him go straight to a 12-bore without bothering with a 16. Some people, especially those of light physique, find that a light 12-bore with 25in barrels is ideal. After years of shooting with 28in barrels I changed to 25in, thinking that the change would help me to shoot really well. It did not do so and I was disappointed, sometimes shooting a lot worse than before. Today my Purdey with 25in barrels, a gun I love dearly, is pensioned off and I shoot with a Spanish gun with normal-length barrels; I shoot better than with the 25in. But many people have experienced exactly the reverse. The answer is to experiment at a shooting school.

When it comes to the boring of the gun I am much more specific. My favourite sport is wildfowling and I have used full choke barrels in the early enthusiasm of youth. Many wildfowlers still use nothing else. My advice is—have them re-bored to improved cylinder in the right and half choke at the most in the left.

A fully choked gun is a great handicap. The good wildfowler is not he who can scrape down a goose or a duck at seventy yards. That is a fluke nine times out of ten. How much better to use one's skill and knowledge to get within reasonable range —and then shoot really well. Wildfowling is a sport of great variety. When conditions are really right, and wigeon or geese are coming fast and in good numbers, then a fully choked weapon is a handicap. For ducks coming to a specific point (for instance, a flight pond) I use No 7 shot. For high passengers I use a short No 7 in the right barrel and a 2¾in No 4, or 3in No 3, in the left. Often I kill more ducks stone dead with the right barrel, and No 7s, than with the heavier load in the left, which may only wing them. For geese I use 3in No 3 in the right and BB in the left. In spite of the fact that on paper the No 3s should give the best pattern and therefore the best results, I find that BB is the most satisfactory. That is simply because I am not a good enough shot to put the centre of the pattern on the head or neck. For those who can do this, nothing larger than No 3 is necessary for geese. I do not now possess a gun with full choke boring and I would not use it at all if I did.

The construction of butts or hides is of absorbing interest. First there is the problem of precise siting, and then there is the problem of making the butt or hide merge into the landscape. Any form of sunken butt is the most efficient, provided it is not full of water. For wildfowl, a hole with a sunken tub that can be baled out with a plastic bucket, or an inflatable rubber dinghy dug into the mud are good. With permanent hides it is best to use local materials which match the surroundings. These materials can be interwoven into sheep netting supported on stakes, or stuffed between two layers of netting, or tied on with binder twine. Norfolk reeds make first-class material for duck butts, but where they are not available rushes or other local vegetation must be used. A very good method is to start with a long length of binder twine, tying in a bunch of vegetation every three inches. This makes a sort of Hawaiian skirt, which can be draped round the hide structure.

When furbishing a hide, remember that dry dead vegetation changes colour. Spruce or pine branches turn bright red-brown before they go grey. Dead grass and rushes are ideal for the winter scene, but they are obvious against green vegetation. Broom is perfect for a background of green vegetation, but ultimately it turns black.

Permanent butts, placed on marshes or land where animals graze, can be demolished the day after they are put up by a herd of awkward bullocks. What is worse than to get up on a dark, rainy morning, and struggle out to the marsh, only to find one's butt demolished? Nothing is more depressing than to be struggling to re-erect some form of cover, whilst ducks are trying to knock one's hat off. Cattle must be kept off by a square of barbed wire, and one corner of the barbed wire should have a sack wrapped round it to protect one's waterproof clothing in the dark.

Many years ago, when lorry-loads of iron bedsteads were available in any big city for the asking, we used the ends as the basis for bullock-proof butts—four wired together and strengthened by stout posts and stuffed with vegetation. However, today they do not seem to be available. Perhaps they have been exported to America as antiques!

Background for concealment is all-important. Anyone suitably clothed—by that I mean someone who is not bald and hatless, and not wearing a yellow oilskin or a white shirt—who remains motionless *in front* of a suitable background stands a good chance of not being seen. Any chameleon, or deer, will confirm that. The best-camouflaged man, standing in a well-built hide, will stick out like a sore thumb if he and the hide are on the skyline.

The human form is difficult to disguise, and wildfowl in particular soon learn to recognise man from the shape of his head and shoulders. In heavily shot areas, even the outline of a man lying prone is quickly recognised.

This brings me to the greatest challenge of all for the rough shooter and wildfowler, that of becoming unseen where there is no cover whatsoever. The art of camouflage is not so much a matter of concealment as one of deception. The quarry will see you, but it must be misled into thinking that you are a natural part of the landscape. If you fail in this you will not get a shot. If you succeed, then you will have the best sport of all: for the best chances at duck and geese are where they fly low, because they think that no fowler could be present. Therefore you must either break up your outline so that it looks too small to be a man, which is difficult, or you must enlarge the outline so that you disappear into part of what looks like something else. This needs a careful study of the background which may be a shingle bank, flat sand, or bare mud. Your camouflage must be a replica, as seen from a distance, and it must look nearly flat as seen from the air. With the many forms of plastic, netting and other fabrics which are available today, this is much less difficult than it used to be. I have tried a score or more different things, several with great success.

I remember on one occasion I was waiting for the geese to flight under the moon on the Solway. I was well hidden, and it was a beautiful still night with the full moon making visibility almost as good as by day. Two fowlers came and sat, side by side, on a mound about 20yd from me. I could hear every word they said and the peace of the merse was shattered. 'Reckon the ducks will be coming soon,' said one. So I quacked softly like a mallard. They looped the loop and took up prone positions, like gunmen in a Western. There was silence for a while. 'Did you see that one?', asked one, and his mate replied, 'No, reckon he must have gone.' They sat up again on the mound and started chattering. I quacked again—and down they went on their faces. After the third time the truth dawned. 'That's some b——r pretending to be a duck. Let's go.' They stumbled away, grumbling, and the peace of the merse was restored. But they never knew where I was. The geese flighted over another part of the saltings and I went home to bed.

On another occasion I had a silly desire to shoot a goose from an armchair. I carried a wicker armchair out on to the open shore and camouflaged it to look like a rock. Unfortunately the geese flighted on a different line. But I had curlew, redshank and dunlin walking past within ten paces—and if you can fool a curlew on the bare sand you can fool anything.

Yet another time I wanted to test the theory that if you put out a large enough object, that can be seen from a mile away, it will not cause alarm. I got an enormous black net, spread it out on bare golden sand, and lay under a corner of it for morning flight. One lot of pinks came straight for me. When they were nearly over the net they were greatly puzzled. They did not swerve away, but with grunting alarm notes started to rise above it. I shot one goose and it fell within a few yards of the edge of the net, but the experiment had failed because it did alarm them. A perfectly camouflaged net, which matched the sand exactly, would have worked perfectly: but that I knew already.

Let those who feel so inclined take up the challenge of camouflage. It is an absorbing interest and when it has been solved a camera, even without a telephoto lens, will be found to be as exciting as a gun, and the bag is more permanent. I carry a camera whenever I go out shooting and on most other occasions.

This year, with the help of a friend, I have at last got the perfect hide for my part of the shore. It can be carried in one hand, erected in thirty seconds, and I *think* it will completely hide both me and the dog. It will replace my old, rather heavy mud hide made in the shape of a horse's hoof. I am getting too old to lug the hoof very far now. But this hide is still on the secret list!

Portable hides for the land are no problem. The most simple portable hide is made of plastic netting (obtained from garden centres) supported by four light stakes or canes and interwoven with broom and grass alternately. It will roll up, and can be tied with a cord (slip knots) at each end and slung over one's back. The last thing to do after putting up a portable hide is to walk out in front of it to see how it looks. Very often a few handfuls of dry grass, just thrown on to it haphazardly, will make it 100 per cent efficient. In fact, if I am hiding behind a sparse bush, bare of leaves in winter, I add a few handfuls of grass to the bare twigs and this will improve the most moderate form of cover.

12
Some Anecdotes

Interesting things are very often seen by shooting men, especially those who remain still in one place. Perhaps the wildfowler doing a tide flight sees most, when there is a continuous movement of bird-life crossing his front, or the roe deer stalker, who is about at dawn, when so many wild creatures are moving about. Thus I have had for company for an hour a very young common seal who could not understand why my black retriever, Bear, was not permitted to take to the water to play with him—nor could Bear for that matter. Another day, when waiting for a duck on the edge of the tide, I saw a herring gull coming towards me carrying a tin can! Its left leg hung limp and lifeless and its foot was firmly fixed in the top of the empty tin, swinging to and fro. No doubt it had got its foot caught at the local rubbish dump. When the gull settled on the water, as it was sure to do, the tin would fill and be a very inconvenient attachment.

I have had a hundred whooper swans, all calling with that wonderful, haunting, fluted sound, which is perhaps the most fitting sound of all for the wide, open mudflats, flight low over my head and settle with a great commotion not very many yards from my hide. When lying motionless in a hole in the saltings, I have had a wren settle on my gun barrels, without knowing that there was a human being within half a mile: a curious incident because a wren is not really a bird of the saltmarsh. And, once, a robin settled on the barrel of my rifle, when I was sitting on a high seat, waiting for a fallow buck. That was during a spell of very hard weather and I thought that the confiding bird did recognise me as a possible source of crumbs: of course I had nothing to give it.

Once again, when lying in a hollow in the saltings, I had an unexpected and unusual companion (unusual for such a situation), which surprised me greatly. For, when the tide came in and washed me out of my hollow, there was a great commotion, and out shot a rather muddy rabbit. He must have known I was there, but I had been completely unaware of his presence.

When waiting for roe I have had a blackcock settle in a larch tree only a few feet above my head. He looked for danger everywhere, except between his feet, and when he was satisfied that there was none, he made a good meal of young larch shoots, which are also a favourite food of caper and roe deer in the early spring. Often, when stalking roe on a lovely May morning, I listen with enormous pleasure to the beautiful spring song of a blackcock. Sometimes, too, I hear a cock caper pretending to withdraw a cork from a bottle—not a very impressive sound for such an impressive bird, but no doubt the sophisticated lady caper appreciate it.

Caper are often seen by the stealthy roe stalker. On one occasion I crawled very slowly and silently up a low bank, hoping to see a buck in the larch wood beyond. To our mutual astonishment I came face to face with a huge cock caper, not six feet away! It was beneath the dignity of such a regal creature to depart over-hastily. With great composure, and very deliberately, he walked away until he was behind a larch tree. Then he took off, remarkably quickly, and kept the tree between my rifle and himself. How was he to know that he was perfectly safe, anyway?

Early one morning I watched a buzzard mobbing a golden eagle. Sometimes one thinks: could that buzzard wheeling in the sky possibly be an eagle? Well, when one sees them together, the enormous disparity in size (a buzzard close to an eagle looks no larger than a kestrel close to a buzzard), makes one realise that it could not be. If there is doubt, then it is a buzzard. There is no doubt when the eagle hangs in the sky, because of his great wingspan, and still less when one realises the great speed with which he passed out of one's ken over the far hill. On motionless wings the eagle has traversed the whole length of the glen. On that morning, when I watched the two birds, they disappeared through a pass in the hills. So I resumed my stalk. A little while later I was walking slowly up a steep bluff, hoping to see a buck beyond the top, when, quite suddenly, the eagle, still accompanied by the buzzard of whose presence he was utterly disdainful, swept low over the bluff. They passed about 30ft above my head.

Many years ago I went up on to a Welsh moor on 10 December, hoping to rid the moor of a few surplus cock grouse. I cannot now remember whether I shot any, but a peregrine falcon stooped out of the sky, like a blue arrow, and knocked down a cock grouse not very far from me. Its head was practically severed from its body, which is usual, the blow being given by the back talon of the falcon.

Once when I was shooting wigeon flighting over a promontory, a tiercel stooped several times at redshank (rather an ignoble prey after a grouse!). Each redshank in turn adopted the same escape tactics and flew so low over the tideway that the falcon could not drive home his stoop without being immersed. No hawk will risk damage to its flight feathers.

Unexpected collisions sometimes occur. Electric power cables take quite a toll. I have known swans, geese, pheasants, grouse, partridges and mallard collide with cables, with fatal results. Once I picked up a snipe on my lawn. It had flown into the telephone wires. The interesting thing was that I had never seen a snipe anywhere near that house.

Once when watching a huge concourse of geese—pinkfeet—circling high above the central Solway flats, I saw a goose falling like a stone. Obviously it had collided with another. It fell 200 or 300ft, and then recovered, slowly winging its way back to join the others. On the whole it is surprising that birds, especially game birds flying in coveys, or packs, do not collide with each other more often.

It always surprises me that more shooting men are not struck by birds which have been shot. I have seen it happen, but not often. I once shot a very tall teal travelling down-wind with a gale in its tail—a satisfactory shot. My companion was working his spaniel a little distance away the other side of a stone wall. The teal fell on the head of the unfortunate dog, who refused to pick it up, or even work any more that morning. I should think that the dog had a splitting headache.

Wounded birds quite often end up in unusual places. One August, when the beaters had almost reached the butts, a single grouse was flushed and I had to take it behind, and wounded it. The lunch hut, where the cars were parked, was some 700 or 800yd away, and although I could not quite see the hut, I knew where it was. The wounded grouse appeared to fly directly towards it. It was found lying under the front bumper of my host's Land Rover, within a few feet of the lunch hut! A friend once shot a goose under the moon as a small skein flew over the Powfoot Hotel, where we were staying, on Solway. Apparently it fell on the roof. Certainly we could not find it in the yard the other side. However, after a search of the roof with ladders the next day, it was still missing. I suspect it found its way into the oven of some local who was passing the back of the hotel at just the right moment.

Cannons, as Peter Hawker called two birds killed by one shot, are not very infrequent. Double cannons are. Three of us were once flighting a pond in Hampshire. On that particular evening it was my turn for the middle butt. Four mallard came first, winging their way across the water-meadow, straight for me. As I mounted my gun to take the leading duck, the one following swerved slightly behind it. They both fell, dead, to the shot. The other two flared up and again crossed as I fired my second barrel. To the surprise of all concerned they fell dead too. There was a moment of hushed silence, and then simultaneous comments came from the butts on each side of me, plaintively: 'You might have left me *one*', and, more emphatically: 'You greedy sod!'

On a cocks-only day, a well-known Shropshire sportsman was heading a long, wooded dingle near Aston-on-Clun. Two pheasants, a cock and a hen, came planing down the dingle on set wings, the cock about six feet in front of the hen. They both fell dead to one shot: a case of the shot charge 'stringing'.

Again in Shropshire, at Felhampton, I was standing next to Sir Rowland Clegg at a small partridge drive. He was outside gun and to his left was a gate in the hedge over which we hoped a covey or two would come. A covey of five flew over the gate. As the leading bird topped the gate he fired—and killed all five birds with the one shot, a remarkable happening.

When shooting in Anglesey I shot at a cock pheasant flying parallel to a small bank. The pheasant was killed, and so was a rabbit of whose presence on the bank I was unaware. On the same very well-known shoot it is recorded that a gun shooting at a cock pheasant missed and bowled over a large turkey cock. As it was Christmas time he was never allowed to live it down.

My first punt shot, also in Anglesey, killed five ducks, which is nothing unusual. The extraordinary thing was that they were of four different species—mallard, teal, wigeon and either a shoveler or a pintail (unfortunately, I cannot now remember which it was).

Unexpectedly amusing incidents are no less frequent in the shooting field than they are in everyday life. We rent a small grouse moor from which we obtain an enormous amount of enjoyment. But the costs of running a grouse moor, where beaters average £50 per day, are very high. Therefore we have to take in one or two paying guns, not for profit, but to help out with our overheads.

I remember the first day of a rather poor season. In spite of all the hard work our wonderful keeper had done, often aided by our own informal butt-building or heather-burning outings, and in spite of a very favourable winter for heather, and grouse, snow at hatching time had caused a disaster to what should have been a record season. How often something like that happens!

So we were not expecting a very good day and our guests had been told that, although I do not know that the Frenchmen understood. The first two drives were reasonably good. Some seventy shots were fired for three brace. The next drive was bad, just a handful of shots from the far end of the line. The oldest Frenchman stamped up to Eric, who was feeling very glum, and, making a circle with his forefinger and thumb just under Eric's nose, exploded verbally: 'Zero, zero—tereebull!' he shouted, and then stomped off, muttering to himself.

Eric and John, considerably taken aback, grinned broadly. At least their despondency was relieved. But at that moment the old boy whipped round and caught them laughing. He stamped back and making a very dramatic mime with his fingers across his own mouth, he said: 'You should not look, so', pulling the corners of his mouth sideways into a horrible grin. 'You should look, so', and he pulled his nose upwards and chin downwards into a hideous scowl, and off he stamped again. Eric just had time to whisper 'For God's sake keep a straight face'—none too soon, for the old boy whirled round again, and with great self-control they managed to look duly sombre for the moment. The last two drives were absolutely disastrous—they produced two grouse and a snipe, the last a very unfortunate bird for, to my certain knowledge, he had not been on that part of the moor on a shooting day for the last three seasons. Speaking for myself, I kept well out of the way of Monsieur Zero on the way back to the cars.

The next day was on the beat, which is not usually the best. However, the first drive produced a few coveys which went over the line, but from my position, flanking, I could not see who had the shooting. So, emboldened by a good night's rest and a lovely sunny day, I went up to our elderly French friend and said 'Did you get a shot?' I might have known. Up came his fingers and thumb. 'Zero,' he said, 'Zero'.

However, at the next drive a grouse would have knocked his hat off, had he been wearing one, and he had some shooting at each subsequent drive. His bag was zero. But after each drive he searched the heather carefully 30yd behind his butt, hoping that by some miracle he might find a grouse that had died of natural causes.

The last drive was an experiment to a new line of butts which I had put up along a fence. Luckily it worked quite well, but our friend Monsieur Zero was out of it. However, we had told him he could shoot hares and presently I saw him let off both barrels at one. He stood with an empty gun watching the hare disappear, no doubt hoping for another miracle: that it would stumble and break its neck. At that moment a single grouse flew low over his head. He was very angry.

When the beaters were within 70yd of the butts, an old cock grouse got up and flew straight for our worthy friend. I said a hasty prayer: 'If he is going to shoot anyone, please don't let it be our very precious keeper', who was roughly opposite him. However, he held his fire and was preparing to turn round to take the grouse behind, when that misguided bird flew into the top wire of the fence, within a yard of his butt, looped the loop, and fell on its backside at his feet. The miracle had happened. Throwing his gun aside the old man pounced on the grouse. With a throaty chuckle, which sounded very like 'zero', that astonishing bird took wing and flew clean away!

Index

Acme whistle, 96
acorn, 127, 135
alder, 53, 57, 78
alpha chlorolose, 117, 123
Amelanchier canadensis, see snowy mespilus
ammonium nitrate, 76
Anglesey, 59
antlers, 86, 87, 88, 91
artichoke, 53
Ascot, 45
ash, 52

badger, 123
bark stripping, 86
barley, 65, 135
'Bear', 39–40, 100
Beauly Firth, 61, 62
beech, 52
beech mast, 127, 135
bilberry (*Vaccinium*), 32, 37
birch, 53, 57
Bird Act 1954, 112
bird cherry, 53
bistort (*Polygonum*), 79
blackgame, 15, 32–9, 53, 146
blasting, 72, 73, 74, 76
boreing (of guns), 140
bracken, 57
British Field Sports Society, 20
broom, 44, 48, 57, 79
'browse line', 85
buckwheat, 53

bulldozer, 72–4
burning (of heather), 23–31
burreed (*Sparganium*), 79
Butts, hides, 19, 35, 63, 70, 96, 134, 140, 141
buzzard, 112, 115–16, 118, 146–7

Caernarvon, 59
camouflage, 138, 141–2
capercaillie, 32, 39–41, 146
cherry, 53; bird cherry, 53
Christmas tree, 47, 52
climate, 15–16
Clocaenog forest, 40
Cornus sibirica (dogwood), 78
Cornwall, 59
Corsican pine, 52, 127
cotoneaster, 77; *erigidus*, 53, 78; *horizontalis*, 79; *Nicrophylla*, 47, 79
cranberry, 37
crossbill, 127
crow, 21, 112, 118, 121
crowfoot, water (*Ranunculus*), 79

dam, 72, 75–6
decoys, 63, 127, 134, 135
deer, 52, 82–91, 99, 103, 109
dogging, 34
dogwood, 77
Douglas fir, 51
doves, 132–3
dragline, 72, 76

INDEX

driving: blackgame, 38; caper, 40; geese, 63; grouse, 35, 114; hares, 131; partridge, 44; snipe, 79
duck, 4, 18, 110
Dyfnant forest, 38
dynamite, 76

eagle, 18, 21, 22, 113, 116, 146
ear plugs, 125
Eire, 59
electric pylons, 44
Elodia crispa, 79
enteromorpha, 62
explosive for blasting ponds, 76–8

fallow deer, 82
farmers, 16, 137
ferreting, 120, 128–30
fieldcraft, 14, 126
fire, 23, 29, 90; fire beaters, 30; firebreak, 28, 29
flanker, 36
flighting, 62, 65, 95, 148
flight ponds, 70
flushing points, 47, 52
Forestry Commission, 46
fox, 21, 22, 89, 99, 121, 122
fraying (deer), 86
French partridge, 16, 40, 105

Galtheria, 47
Game Conservancy, 20, 45
game larder, 14
geese: bean, 60; brent, 62; canada, 61, 62; grey, 62; greylag, 60, 61, 62; pinkfoot, 61, 62; white fronted, 61, 62
gelignite, 76
gizzard, 15, 32
goosander, 112
gorse, 44, 57, 58

goshawk, 114, 115
grey hen, 38
grit, 15, 32
grouse, 14, 21–36, 60, 108, 114, 116
gulls, 112, 145
guns, choice of, 139–40

hare, 15, 52, 85, 99, 109, 131, 132; blue, 22, 131
harrier, 114
heather, 21–38
hemlock, western (*Tsuga*), 47, 57
hides, *see* butts
high seat, 88–91, 145
holly, 57
hornbeam, 78

Inverness, 61
Islay, 59

jackdaw, 96, 112, 118, 121
Japanese pheasant, 15
jay, 96, 112
juniper, 48

kale, 45, 53, 54, 135
kestrel, 112, 115, 116

Lake District, 40
Lake Vyrnwy, 38
Land Rover, 26
larch, 51, 57
laurel, 47, 57
lek, 39
Lleyn, 59
lodge-pole, pine (*Pinus contorta*), 38, 52
lonicera, 47
lupin, tree, 48, 79

magpie, 96, 112, 118, 121
mallard, 10, 61, 63

INDEX

mangold, 43
marshland, 3, 60, 79
master eye, 125
merganser, 112
mink, 123
Minster Lovell, 18
Molinia (ribbon grass), 24, 25
moorhen, 66
mountain ash, 37, 53
Mull, 59
Mull of Galloway, 59
Mull of Kintyre, 59
muntjac, 82, 87

Neusiedler Sea, 60
New Forest, 89
Norfolk reed (*Phragmites*), 60, 79
Northern Ireland, 59
Norway spruce, 47, 51
Nothofagus, 52

oak, 52, 104, 128
oat (stubble), 38
open season: blackgame, 37; caper, 41; deer, 83; duck, 64; geese, 64; grouse, 64; snipe, 64; woodcock, 55
Orkney, 59
otter, 123
owl, 112, 115, 116; stuffed, 118

partridge, 15, 42–5, 54, 60, 106, 108, 109, 115
Pembrokeshire, 59
peregrine, 114
pheasant, 15, 45–55, 60, 95, 108, 116
Phragmites, see Norfolk reed
picking-up, 66, 106
pigeon, 20, 107, 108, 115, 120, 126, 132–7
pointers, 34

polecat, 123
Polygonum, see bistort
pond, feeding of, 66; making, 70–9
poplar, 52, 78
potatoes, 43, 62
predation, 33, 54, 88, 89, 98, 112, 113
ptarmigan, 18, 21, 114

rabbit, 15, 52, 85, 103, 104, 109, 115, 126
rape (plant), 45, 135
rat, 123, 131
raven, 112, 118
red deer, 21, 23, 82, 87, 88
red oak, 52
rhododendron, 57
ribbon grass, see Molinia
rifle, calibre, 83
roding, 56
roe deer, 15, 20, 56, 60, 61, 82, 83, 87, 122
rook, 112, 118
root vegetables, 42–4, 62
Rousay, 59
rushes, 25, 32
rut, 123, 131

safety, 126
sallow, 48
saltmarshes, 62, 80
scent, 96–100
Scots pine, 36, 52, 127
sea buckthorn, 48, 78
shooting dogs, 92–102; clumber spaniel, 94; curly coat retriever, 93; dachshund, 92; English springer spaniel, 93, 119; flat-coat retriever, 93; fox terrier, 92, 122; German pointer, 93–4; Irish water spaniel, 93; labrador, 93, 94, 101, 102; pointer, 34,

INDEX

shooting dogs—*cont.*
  93; retriever, 93; setter, 34, 93; Weinerama, 93–4; Welsh springer spaniel, 93; vizsla, 93–4
shotgun, 82, 139
shot sizes, 82, 140
sika deer, 60
sitka spruce, 51
slots (deer), 84, 85
snaring, 130
snipe, 15, 64, 96, 105, 107, 108, 119
snow, 22, 58, 62
snowy mespilus (*Amelanchier canadensis*), 53, 78
soil, types of, 15; alkaline silt, 79; base rich, 32, 52, 72; clay, 15; peat, 73; porous, 72; sandy loam, 15
squirrel grey, 52, 53, 123, 126, 127
SSG shot, 82
stoat, 123
stops, 54
stubble, 42, 62
sugar beet, 43
swans, 103, 145
swedes, 43
sweet chestnut, 53
sycamore, 53, 128

teal, 10, 61
territorial behaviour, grouse, 33; roe, 83

Thetford Chase, 40
thumbstick, 87
tides, 80
topography, 16
towering (birds), 107
trout, 15, 72, 75
Tsuga, *see* hemlock, western
Turkey oak, 52
turnips, 43, 62

Vaccinium, *see* bilberry
vermin control, 17, 45, 112–23
vizsla, 93
vole, 115, 121

walking up, 34
Warfarin, 123
weasel, 123
wheat, 62, 66, 104, 135
whinchat, 39
wigeon, 10, 61
wild boar, 61, 99, 131
wild cat, 22, 118, 122
wildfowl, 5
Wildfowl Association of Great Britain and Ireland, 20, 59
willow, 78
wind direction, 24, 26
woodcock, 15, 46, 55–9, 96, 104, 108
woodpecker, greater spotted, 127

zostera, 62